Anatomy of a Streetfight

By Paul Vunak

ttp

First published in 2001 by
Unique Publications, Inc.

Disclaimer

ISBN: 0-86568-187-2
Library of Congress Catalog Number: 2001 131958

Distributed by:
Unique Publications
4201 Vanowen Place
Burbank, CA 91505
(800) 332-3330

First edition
05 04 03 02 3 5 7 9 10 8 6 4 2

Printed in the United States of America

Editor: Dave Cater
Design: George Foon

Dedication

I would like to dedicate this book to my guru, mentor, and friend, Dan Inosanto.

Acknowledgements

First and foremost, I would like to thank my wife, Erin, for her help writing, compiling, organizing, and editing. If not for her, this book would not be in your hands until the next millennium!

Very special thanks to Larkin Fourkiller, Michael Holsapple, and Bruce Aukerman for their tremendous contributions.

About the Author

Paul Vunak is the President and Founder of Progressive Fighting Systems, and trainer of the United States Navy SEAL teams.

He is currently working with the DEA, FBI, and over 50 police departments throughout the country.

Progressive Fighting Systems has over 200 instructors representing 4,000 students worldwide. Mr. Vunak can be reached at **www.fighting.net**

Table of Contents

Preface

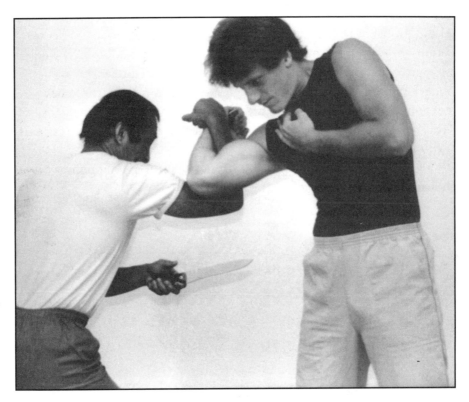

"If you want to understand the truth in martial arts, to see any fight clearly, you must throw away the notion of styles or schools, prejudices, likes and dislikes, and so forth. Then, your mind will cease all conflict and come to rest. In this silence, you will see totally and freshly."

— Bruce Lee

Let's first discuss and define the meaning behind *Anatomy of a Streetfight*. What is a streetfight? If we were to take a worldwide survey and ask, "Who is the best fighter on the planet?" it would quickly become obvious the difference in perception. The average American would probably pick his favorite heavyweight boxer, perhaps Mike Tyson. (However, the question was not "who is the best boxer?") The average Filipino would probably answer, "Floro Villabrille." (A legendary stick/blade master, but the question was not "who is the best weapons fighter?") Ask the question in Brazil, and the answer might be "Rickson Gracie" or "Rigan Machado." (However, the question was not "who is the best groundfighter?")

So, I ask again, what exactly is a streetfight? It is any random act of violence, period!

While this definition includes kicking, punching, stick- and knife-fighting, and groundfighting, it does not preclude two-on-one, three-on-one, four-on-two, pinching, biting, eye gouging, firearms, carjackings, and all-out riots.

I titled this book *Anatomy of a Streetfight* for a reason. It is not about tradition; it is not about styles or systems. It is not about sports, or tournaments, and certainly not about rules. My objective is to introduce the "rigid rod of reality." Violence cannot be contained within a neat little package. It is not to be taken lightly and certainly not to be romanticized. This book clarifies some issues that have previously been clouded, sparks some questions that should be asked, and ultimately fills in a hole and completes the puzzle.

CHAPTER 1

No-Holds-Barred Tournaments are not Streetfights

The last ten years of martial arts have seen more growth and progress than the previous fifty, because of the insurgence of the many no-holds-barred tournaments occurring worldwide. My respect and admiration for these warriors goes beyond words. They are among the toughest, most well-conditioned athletes on the planet. We see the quality of fighters improving each year. These fighters are becoming more complete every day. Punchers and kickers are learning to grapple, and grapplers are slowly learning to punch and kick. Being well-rounded and multidimensional are no longer just trendy ideas, but downright necessities.

Although they may not realize it, these fighters are truly harvesting the seeds that were planted by Bruce Lee and Dan Inosanto in the 1970s. All one has to do is pick up *The Tao of Jeet Kune Do*, and it becomes obvious that the principles and concepts the two discovered are being implemented to a "T."

Unfortunately, many people are confusing NHB tournaments with streetfights. When a fighter enters a NHB competition, there is an element of control over many aspects of the fight. A competitor is given several months to train and get in the best possible shape. Conversely, in the street, one is forced to confront violence with absolutely no control over where, when, how, or why the fight will ensue. Some of this confusion between tournaments and streetfights is a problem of semantics regarding the true definition of a "streetfight." For the sake of clarity, let us use the analogy of a maximum-security prison. Imagine the myriad possible violent encounters that could take place behind those walls (e.g., mass attacks (two-on-one or three-on-one), knifefights, ambushes, makeshift weapons of every possible size and configuration, biting, eye gouging, or just plain mayhem.

Complicating matters further is that many of these scenarios usually end up mutating. Now things become exponentially more difficult. By mutating, I mean changing from one scenario to another within the same fight. For example, the altercation may start off one-on-one standing up and then go to the ground. If another individual jumps in we have a two-on-one fight. Then perhaps two more people enter the equation, giving us a three-on-two situation. At this point someone might grab a pipe — now this has turned into a weapons fight. In retaliation, someone else may grab a blade. Now the scenario has changed to a knifefight. These mutations could potentially be endless. The first thing that comes to mind when talking about being a streetfighter is that one must be highly skilled not only in stand-up and groundfighting, but also with mass-attack scenarios and with all types of weapons — sticks, knives, etc. (According to law enforcement statistics, eight out of ten streetfights involve weapons!)

"You will train the way you fight and fight the way you train."

The next attribute in our quest to become a complete streetfighter is keeping a cool head while these mutations occur. Controlling one's emotions is one of the most essential aspects of a fight. There are moments in the midst of battle where one must "turn on" his killer instinct. There are other moments when controlling the emotions means relaxing and breathing. This is when you are in the moment I like to call the "Fog of War." If one is not highly trained in all areas of combat (i.e., stick, knife, stand-up, ground), and a scenario occurs you have never experienced, panic occurs and controlling your emotions is impossible.

Most people in martial arts are too specialized in their "way" of fighting. For example, if a person's "way" is stickfighting, and he loses his stick, he would certainly be in trouble. If a person's "way" is kickboxing and he ends up on the ground he would also be in trouble. If a person's "way" is groundfighting and he has to fight more than one person, he also would be in trouble. This is why Bruce Lee espoused the rather esoteric axiom of "using no way as way."

Some schools out there are "eclectic" in that they train in many of the aforementioned areas. However, the problem is that they have a tendency to simply compartmentalize these areas. They have a 4 p.m. stick class, a 5 p.m. kickboxing class, a 6 p.m. groundfighting class, and so on. This sort of training does not promote flowing and adapting to the various possible mutations of a streetfight. In boxing, this would be akin to having a 4 p.m. jab class, a 5 p.m. cross class, and a 6 p.m. hook class.

Having classes compartmentalized like this is not in itself a bad thing, provided you follow guro Dan Inosanto's methodology — have one class at your school that combines everything. Guro Dan has always taught me that you will train the way you fight and fight the way you train.

The following illustrates 20 of the most important ways to train for the "anything-can-happen" streetfight.

GUIDE TO TRAINING JKD ATTRIBUTES

- Attribute
- Definition
- Training
- Methodology

1. Awareness
To see the opponent's intentions.
Knife sparring, mixed sparring (one side uses jab only, the other uses all tools).

2. Sensitivity
To feel the opponent's intentions.
Hubbud (Filipino energy drill), chi sao, etc.

3. Proper Mental Attitude
Combination of calm, killer instinct, and confidence
Full-contact training (with loud abusive language), use of vivid imagery during training.

4. Body Mechanics
Knowing how and where to position the body at all times; using no wasted motion.
Weapons training of all types (forces one to exaggerate and emphasize body mechanics).

5. Strength
Ability to overwhelm an opponent through manipulation.
Weight training, wrestling, isometrics, swimming, gymnastics, surfing.

6. Footwork
Putting oneself where one needs to be at all times by shuffling forward and back, sidestepping and circling.
Knife sparring (long range), empty-hand sparring (jab only), jumping rope, running bleachers.

7. Speed
Perception of initiation and performance of an action.

Break any motion into three equal parts (from chambered position to impact) and work each part separately. Also stick sparring.

8. Power
Combination of strength and speed (ability to use your strength quickly).

Heavy bag work, isometrics, wrestling, throwing shot put, full-contact sparring (w/proper gear).

9. Timing
Ability to launch an attack at the proper moment.

Knife sparring (decreasing speed by 50 percent increases need for timing by 50 percent).

10. Coordination
Performing a movement with efficiency, ease and balance.

Double-stick training, focus gloves, cross-training in any physical sport; repetition of desired motion.

11. Balance
Correct body alignment during motion (controlling one's center of gravity).

Most physical sports, especially surfing, water and snow skiing, high kicking, gymnastics.

12. Spatial Relationships
Control over distances (range).

Mixed-weapons sparring using weapons of different ranges (e.g., staff vs. single stick, double-stick vs. knife, etc.).

13. Agility
Being light on one's feet with limberness and quickness.

Gymnastics and dance, knife sparring, handball.

14. Stamina
Combined endurance and wind.

Wrestling, Thai boxing drills, heavy bag work, running, sparring, high kicking.

15. Conditioning
Taking punishment to hands, stomach, thighs, skins.

Mook jong (wooden dummy), Thai boxing drills, shin kicks to heavy bag, straw pad.

17. Rhythm

Deals with faking, cadence breaks, changing tempos, etc.
Double-sticks, conga playing, dancing, speed bag work.

18. Precision

Accuracy and exactness in the projection of force.
Hitting a paper dangling from a string; hitting small targets (use a felt pen) on the heavy bag.

19. Explosiveness

Relaying destructiveness in a sudden manner.
Wrestling, weight training (clean and jerk), heavy bag, and tackle football.

20. Flow

Combination of awareness and sensitivity; uninterrupted concentration.
Stick training (counter drills), empty-hand drills in which one continues through a series of movements without stopping.

A GUIDE TO TRAINING JEET KUNE DO ATTRIBUTES

We have already established that adapting during the many potential transitions is critical. Therefore, to prepare yourself for the street, your training has to mimic all potential mutations that might possibly occur.

For example, start your practice session by stickfighting, then drop your stick, pull out a blade, and continue the match knifefighting. Throw down the blade and continue with kickboxing; then enter into trapping range, implementing headbutts, elbows, and knees. Next, take the fight to the ground and kick into Brazilian jiu-jitsu. Look for the appropriate time to use kina mutai (uninterrupted biting and eye gouging). At this point you could throw another student into the fray — instantly come to your feet and continue the fight as a mass attack. This entire round should flow with no interruptions. Training in this manner emphasizes some of the most vital attributes for a streetfight: Adapting and controlling the emotions during transitions.

I would like to re-emphasize the incredible respect I have for the competitors of NHB tournaments. Their conditioning and focus are at an uncommon level. In fact, they are so focused that this could be detrimental in an actual streetfight. I have borne witness to this firsthand. Indulge me for a moment while I share with you an experience from a day in 1990.

It was a typical Friday afternoon. My partner, Tom Cruse, and I had just finished working with one of the Navy SEAL teams. As tradition would have it, the guys would take us out to their favorite hangout to have a few beers. Our motley crew consisted of three Navy men, Tom, and myself. Our three buddies were all former heavyweight wrestlers of Olympic caliber, with the approximate build of a Mark Coleman or a Mark Kerr. When we arrived at the bar, it looked like something out of a movie: A stereotypical biker bar. My visceral response was to say, "Guys, let's just go home... this place looks like a fight waiting to happen."

But, I knew I had Tom on one side and I glanced over at my three buddies (which translated into about 900 pounds of beef) and thought to myself, "So what — if we fight, we fight." (That was my mentality in those days.) That was **Scene One**.

Scene Two, a couple of hours later, Tom is pulling a typical Tom Cruise in *The Color of Money*, running the pool table and irritating bikers right and left. Finally the whole bar goes into what one could only call a "huddle," and out steps the kingpin biker, a pool player from Hell.

Scene Three. Cruse now has a few hundred dollars of this guy's money, my wrestling buddies are at the other side of the bar talking to some women, and I am grimly assessing the situation. I'm thinking... "I've seen this movie before." At this point, the two pool players are down to their last game and Tom has a straight-in shot on the 9-ball to win the match. Instead of simply making the shot and going home a winner, Tom looks over at me, makes some wisecrack about, "Einstein taught me this," and makes a triple bank and buries it.

To say that the already-volatile situation had reached critical mass would be a slight understatement. We now had about 20 bikers against the five of us. Fists, bottles, and chairs started flying. The three heavyweight wrestlers, all in unison like some synchronized swim show, focused in on one guy apiece, and, in a state of rage took them straight to the ground. This left Tom and me to deal with the rest of the bar! This was one of the worst beatings I have ever taken. In fact, all five of us ended up in the hospital. I personally got the worst of the deal and spent four days in intensive care. It is important to emphasize here that each one of those wrestlers would have done exceptionally well in any NHB tournament.

"This wasn't a no-holds-barred tournament. This was the street."

Here is the moral to the story: This wasn't a no-holds-barred tournament. This was the street.

CHAPTER 2

Rapid Assault Tactics

There is so much contained within the vessel that is jeet kune do it would take a person an entire lifetime to experience it all. It has been my personal goal (during more than 20 years of teaching) to put the most functional aspects of JKD into a format that can be easily absorbed by the average individual. I originally developed this program for our East Coast Navy SEALs (they have so little time to allocate to martial arts, I was forced to streamline the most important elements into a formula that could be learned very quickly). Subsequently, I discovered that many other government agencies have enjoyed this program as well.

HAVE A GAME PLAN

In the world of professional sports, athletes spend surprisingly little time on their game skills (like shooting baskets, catching passes, etc.), and more time on developing, learning, and running specific plays. A National Football League coach would never send his team into the Super Bowl without a game plan. You should have the same approach to self-defense. Possessing skills and techniques alone aren't enough; you need to have an agenda. The first few moments of an attack, when the adrenaline starts pumping and your heart starts racing, is not the appropriate time to try to formulate a defensive strategy! You need a game plan that you can practice ahead of time so in the event of a crisis, you will be able to instinctively do what it takes to survive.

OUR GAME PLAN: THE RAT SYSTEM
(Rapid Assault Tactics)

Angelo Dundee, trainer of the legendary Muhammad Ali, once proclaimed, "The first-est with the most-est is the best-est!" He understood that perhaps the single most-important attribute one could possess in an all-out streetfight is overwhelming one's opponent. And by "overwhelming" I do not mean just physically blasting through someone, but overwhelming him emotionally as well. This means we are going to rattle this opponent — cause him to flinch, shut his eyes, cover up, and perhaps turn away. Once this occurs, the rest of the fight gets exponentially easier.

"The first-est with the most-est is the best-est!"

The difficulty of any streetfight lies in that zone where both fighters are trading blows. This is when you are most vulnerable, especially if your opponent is larger and stronger. The ability to "turn on" a sudden burst of firepower, assaulting your opponent as rapidly as possible, is an indispensable asset.

The principles of rapid assault tactics come directly from Bruce Lee. Although he never formally promoted this systematic approach to an altercation (it just came naturally to him), we have only to examine his tactics when he considered a fight to be serious to see these principles in action.

One of Bruce Lee's greatest assets was the way he began an encounter in a seemingly complete state of relaxation and then suddenly erupted in movement almost too fast for the eye to see. In a fight, Bruce would intercept his opponent before he could even finish launching his blow. This interception would typically be a quick shot to the eyes, knees or groin and would prevent any trading of blows. He would then follow up with a modified version of wing chun's straight blast — a series of straight vertical punches rolling down the opponent's centerline. This happened so quickly the opponent ended up flapping his arms and backpedaling furiously, sometimes on one leg. Bruce jokingly used to refer to the helpless recipient of the powerful straight blast as a "wounded crane."

When a person is on the receiving end of a straight blast, one thing is certain: He has no base and no balance, which are two mandatory factors for any style to be effective. The art of wing chun was developed by a woman, no doubt smaller and not as strong as her male counterparts.

"Once someone is running backward, he is transformed from a martial artist into a simple pedestrian!"

Bruce Lee's friends from China included wing chun stylists Hawkins Cheung (above) and William Cheung (right).

The underlying premise of using wing chun is that you are fighting a bigger, stronger opponent. Trading kicks and punches is clearly not the ideal strategy. The best way to mitigate the size differential is to apply forward pressure to get your opponent backpedaling.

Picture taking a worldwide tour to find the best representative of each and every martial art style. Imagine finding the best tae kwon do person, the best kenpo karate practitioner, the best kung-fu sifu, for example. Each individual has a style of fighting and each possesses his respective attributes. Now, picture these people running backward, frantically trying to stay upright and getting out of the way of fists flying at their faces. Can you then imagine these people trying to pull off their techniques?

Dan Inosanto's "absorb what is useful" philosophy aids the exchange of ideas from all martial arts and martial artists. Bill Wallace (top left), Francis Fong (above right), Eric Lee (above) Inosanto seminar (right).

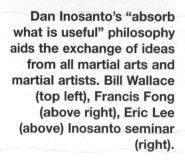

It is an immutable principle that is not affected by style or skill level: Once someone is running backward, he is transformed from a martial artist into a simple pedestrian! It's safe to say that no one practices his art while running backward; however, before you start a new "backward training" program, remember that it's not the reversed direction, but rather the lack of base and balance, that renders the straight blast recipient ineffective.

It's ironic that most people's perception of how Bruce Lee fought has undoubtedly been fostered by his movies. On film, his theatrical jeet kune do was incredibly fun, fancy, and highly entertaining; in reality, Bruce's movement was simple, economical, and direct. Dan Inosanto has said, "Every fight that I have ever seen Bruce in when he was serious, he would straight blast."

After Bruce died in 1973, the responsibility of keeping JKD alive and growing (never static) was conferred upon Dan. Although we read in the *Tao of Jeet Kune Do* about the effectiveness of headbutts, knees, and elbows, the truth is that all of Bruce's fights ended right after the straight blast! Because of his superior attributes, he could execute the blast so flawlessly that he never needed to follow up with an elbow or a knee strike.

Left to right: Ted Lucay Lucay, Dan Inosanto, Paul Vunak and Fred Degerberg.

Obviously, there are few others in this world who possess similar abilities; most of us need everything that Bruce and Dan discovered! As Dan grew in his pursuit of the Filipino martial arts, he discovered how incredibly functional and destructive, and how natural it was to finish off the straight blast with a barrage of elbows, headbutts, and knees. With the addition of these tools to the JKD cocktail, Bruce's already super-effective art became even better.

AN OVERVIEW

I have broken down a fight into three phases, each of equal importance. I will explain what each phase is, and the methods for implementing each phase's tactics. First, we have to enter. If we do not enter in a streetfight, we cannot get into the most lethal range to terminate the fight — where we can use our headbutts, knees and elbows. Everything starts from the entry. Most martial artists kick and punch or grapple. When they're in long range they're going to be throwing bombs at us. We absolutely don't want to trade bombs with people; it will not work, especially if our opponent is larger and stronger. It doesn't matter what style he practices — hard style, soft style, circular, linear — we cannot trade bombs. To enter, we have to either intercept or destroy. An interception and a destruction have one thing in common: inflicting instantaneous pain.

"Once you got your opponent running backward, he has lost all ability to hurt you."

Once our opponent has been subjected to the pain of an interception or destruction, we then go into pressure. Pressure is possibly the most important facet of our game plan. The pressure comes from the art of wing chun and borrows from a technique called the jik chun choy, or straight blast. One of Bruce Lee's biggest revelations was that once your opponent is running backward, he has lost all ability to hurt you. Now that our opponent feels this incredible pressure (the 50-yard dash down his centerline), it is time to terminate the fight. This is accomplished by using the three most barbaric tools on the human body: the knees, the elbows, and the headbutt, which will instantly render an attacker useless.

RAT SYSTEM CHART

• ENTRY	• PRESSURE	• TERMINATION
Interception	Straight Blast	HKE
Destruction		Head
		Knees
		Elbows

Now that you have an overview of the whole game plan, let's look at each phase in greater detail.

PHASE 1: ENTRY

Although there are thousands of martial art styles, all fight within the confines of four ranges: kicking, punching, trapping, and grappling. Bruce Lee and Dan Inosanto discovered back in the 1960s that 99.9 percent of all martial artists fought well in the kicking, punching, and grappling ranges. Very few, however, knew how to fight in trapping range. Our first goal, therefore, is to enter past kicking and punching range, and get into the range which is probably totally unfamiliar to our opponent — trapping range. At this range we are close enough to the opponent to be out of danger from most kicks and punches, and we're close enough to use our most destructive tools (elbows, knees, and headbutts).

Of course, it's highly unlikely that our opponent will let us just "walk in" and start trapping, so the entry — the way we choose to get into trapping range — is important. There are many techniques that make it possible to enter: blocking, ducking, slipping, bobbing, weaving, parrying, for example. The problem is that all these "entries" are passive. You may be able to sneak into trapping range this way, but your opponent will undoubtedly be aware that you're coming and get back out; or worse, he'll be able to catch you with a left hook.

Bruce Lee found the best way to distract an opponent and get in close was to inflict pain. The person would be so focused on whatever body part was in pain, that Bruce would come in and straight blast with total impunity. His preferred method of entry was an interception, which inflicted pain even before his attacker could finish launching a blow. Two examples of an interception would be a finger jab to the eyes or a kick to the groin, executed while the attacker is still in motion. Interceptions are most easily pulled off against an opponent who telegraphs his motions (e.g., a wild "haymaker" swing). They can be difficult against a trained fighter, however; for this reason we also use destructions as entries.

The concept of destructions (which come from the Filipino art of kali) involves attacking the limb that is attacking you. Treat the attack as a target, not a weapon.

PHASE 2: PRESSURE

Our second tactic is pressure – the straight blast. This was one of Bruce Lee's biggest revelations, and is perhaps the most important facet of our game plan. The straight blast turns martial artists into pedestrians! Everybody looks the same when he is running backward. He has no base, no form, and no balance. The straight blast renders any art impotent. Remember: if we do not straight blast an opponent, he'll have his balance — and we'll be in a fight! But you can't just arbitrarily come in, roll your fists and try to straight blast somebody in a fight. You have to first enter with the interception or destruction. Why? Because we need to cause pain first — we then borrow that moment when our opponent is in pain to climb down his centerline with the blast. He is not primed for the big blast.

> "If we do not straight blast an opponent, he'll have his balance – and we'll be in a fight!"

PHASE 3: TERMINATION

As previously mentioned, terminating a fight involves three basic tools — the knees, elbows, and headbutts. Simply put, these are the most barbaric and effective tools for quickly ending an altercation. But while you are applying these tools, you must be clinching onto the back of your opponent's neck (much like a Thai boxer). From this position you not only can launch your knees, headbutts and elbows with maximum power and economy of motion, but you can also ensure that your opponent is trapped right where you want him to be! One other advantage of the neck clinch is that it's a simple matter to rake the opponent's eyes with your thumbs and then return to this position without wasting any time or effort.

When you hold your opponent with a firm grip on his neck, he cannot get back outside to kickboxing range. Nor can he take you to the ground, provided you keep your elbows in centerline and keep up the barrage of headbutts, knees and elbows. Our opponent is now destined to finish the fight in our range — trapping range.

Paul Vunak (left) assumes a ready stance against his attacker, Jeff Clancy (1). Jeff jabs, Paul counters with an arm destruction from the Filipino martial arts (2). Paul follows with an oblique kick to Jeff's shin (3) and backfist to the face, which Jeff blocks (4). Paul attacks the midsection with a round kick from savate (5) and a thigh kick from muay Thai (6).

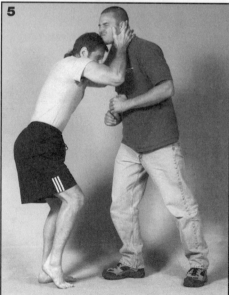

Paul faces his opponent Eric Berger (1). Paul uses his knee for a destruction against a roundhouse (2). Paul straight blasts his opponent (3), then grabs the neck (4) and delivers a headbutt (5).

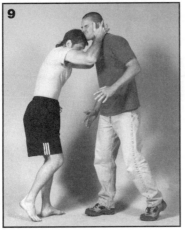

Paul follows up by pushing the opponent's head backward (6) and rakes his elbow across the opponent's throat (7-8). An alternate follow-up after the headbutt (9) can be a knee strike to the groin (10) and knee strike to the temple (11).

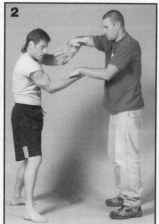

THIS SEQUENCE DEPICT ENERGY DRILLS.
Chi sao, an energy drill from wing chun with opponent Eric Berge (1-2). Paul applies different trapping techniques from the chi sao *drill. Pak sao (3-5). Jaw sao (6-8).*

Chun chuie (9-10). Inside strike (11). Elbow strike (12). Arm wrench (13),

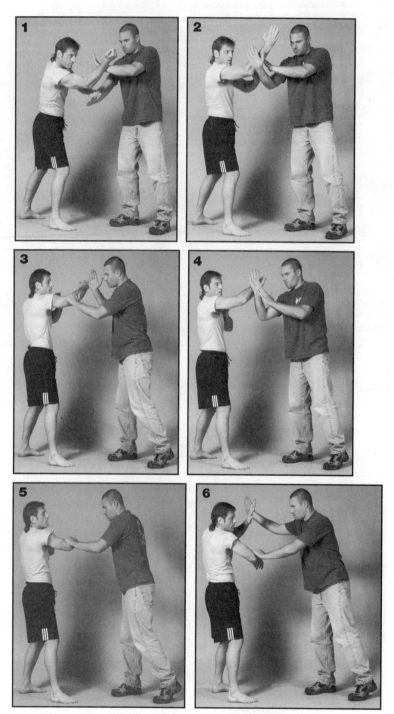

This series illustrates hubbud, *an energy drill from the Filipino martial arts (1-6).*

Using hubbud, Paul deflects opponent's arm across his own body and delivers a downward hammerfist to the arm (1-3).

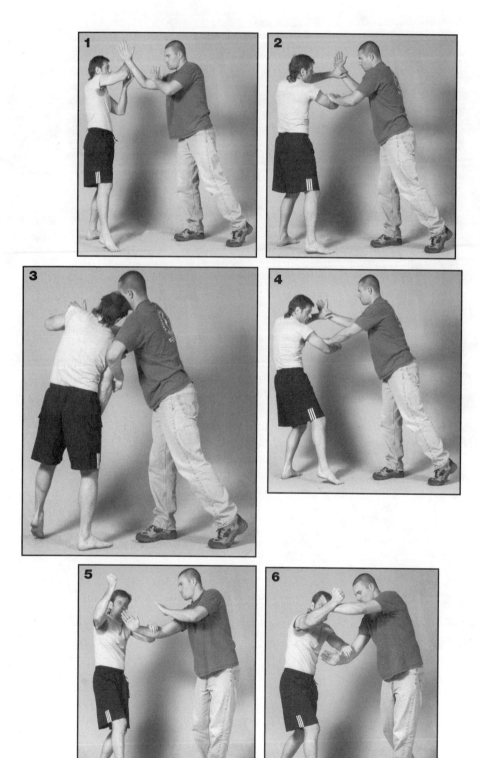

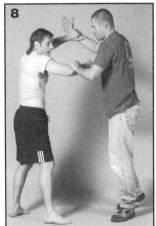

From hubbud drill (1), Paul traps the opponent's arms, pulling them downward (2). Opening the high line for a headbutt (3). Maintaining the energy drill (4), Paul traps the opponent's arms from the other side (5-6) and inserts a headbutt (7). Continuing the energy drill (8), Paul waits until the low line is open and delivers a knee strike to the groin (9). From the energy drill (10), Paul delivers a knee strike to opponent's thigh (11).

In the example above, Paul attempts a low cross, which the opponent blocks (1). Paul does a pak sao to trap the arm and throws a backfist, gua choie (2). When the opponent blocks the high backfist (3), Paul puts in a pin choie (low jab), which the opponent attempts to block with his rear hand (4). Paul traps the rear hand (5).....

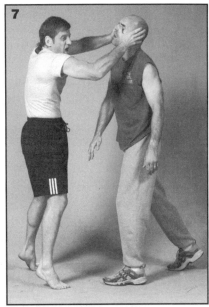

..... and delivers a straight punch to the face (6). He uses his thumbs to rake the opponent's eyes (1) and grabs his neck for a headbutt (8).

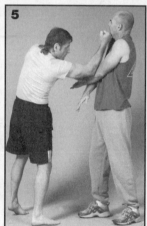

FLOW PATTERN USING A MULTITUDE OF ARTS.

Paul (left) launches into a straight blast from wing chun (1-2), which Jeff counters by blocking with his forearm (3). Paul traps Jeff's front arm with a pak sao and punches. Jeff blocks the punch with his rear hand (4). Paul uses a lop sao to trap the arm and lands a backfist to Jeff's face (5). Paul attacks the bicep with an elbow using Filipino kali (6), followed by an upward arm wrench (7). He then drops low to deliver a groin shot (8). Paul steps in close to his opponent (9)...to prepare for tai chi sail (10).

CHAPTER 3

Killer Instinct

Defining killer instinct is difficult. So much has been postulated, written, and discussed on the subject, but when it comes right down to it, it's impossible to describe in 100 words or less! Killer instinct is the desire and ability to finish your opponent. It's not about twisting your face into ugly expressions or how loudly you scream expletives at your attacker. And it is certainly not mindlessly hurling yourself into the fray with an uncontrolled rush of adrenaline. Killer instinct is finishing the race, closing the deal, accomplishing the mission.

Killer instinct is the correct choice of tactics and the merciless, relentless application of those tactics. It is every choice and action that leads to the downfall of your opponent. It's an attribute, but it is also a mentality.

Firm-gripped control over our most intense emotions is a hallmark of killer instinct. If we are to fully realize the maximum potential of our killer instinct, we cannot be a slave to our emotions. Think of any predator and the manner in which he stalks his prey (a cheetah, for example). It may not have eaten for several days, but it will still wait patiently for the appropriate moment to attack. Its nourishment depends on its skill as a hunter, so it is only logical that it would be quite proficient at this task. One aspect of its skill (an aspect that is easy to overlook) is patience. It knows, innately or by experience, that if it allows a nagging belly to impair its judgment, it will only have to wait longer for its next meal. So the cheetah calmly waits while collecting data that will shape its attack plan. Which gazelle will be the easiest victim? Which gazelle will stray into range first? When the appropriate moment arrives, the cheetah unhesitatingly launches its attack, mercilessly closing on its target with single-minded determination. There is no anger, no emotion in the cheetah. It simply tears its victim down in the most efficient manner possible, not stopping until the struggle is over. This is the epitome of killer instinct.

> "There is no anger, no emotion in the cheetah. It simply tears its victim down in the most efficient manner possible, not stopping until the struggle is over."

There is a vast wealth of knowledge to be gained from studying predatory animals. If you compare the jeet kune do game plan with that of the cheetah, you will find many similarities. In the embryonic stages of a streetfight, we make our preliminary analysis. This will include any observations about our adversary's structure (boxer, karate man, wrestler, etc.). Our preliminary analysis must be as accurate as possible, because tactical choices will be made from this data. It cannot be tainted by too much emotion.

Just as the cheetah looks for the weakest gazelle, we look for any apparent weakness in our opponent's defense. It would not be particularly wise for the cheetah to hunt the strongest, fastest gazelle; nor would it make sense for us to try to outbox a stronger, faster boxer. In our case, we don't stand around waiting for an opportunity, but try to create one by moving and probing. Through this process we can get the opponent to reveal much more about himself than he would probably like, and possibly even make a mistake. When the time is right we enter, straight blast, and finish our opponent with an unrelenting barrage of headbutts, knees and elbows. This is the point of no return. We must assume that our survival depends upon the success of this technique, and our emotional intensity must reflect this belief.

"We have to go from a cold, unfeeling machine to a raging grizzly bear and back again in a second if the situation calls for it."

To reach the full potential of our killer instinct, we must control our emotional make-up. We have to go from a cold, unfeeling machine to a raging grizzly bear and back again in a second if the situation calls for it. In kicking and punching range, we must be that machine, free from any emotional tension or anxiety. We dispassionately view the situation and react to it as if it were a blatantly obvious course of action. Once we enter into trapping range, we must become a wild animal, oblivious to pain or reason. If the fight goes to the ground, we must kick back into machine mode so we can effectively make the correct tactical decisions.

There is a common misconception that someone who angers easily or "blows his top" regularly has a lot of "killer instinct." Not true. This is simply a person who is being led around by his emotions. To me it's like a little kid having a temper tantrum! Legendary basketball coach Phil Jackson, in his book *Sacred Hoops*, talks about emotional control: "It was no coincidence that the players had a hard time staying focused against

Detroit. The Pistons' primary objective was to throw us off our game by raising the level of violence on the floor…I realized that anger was the Bulls' real enemy, not the Detroit Pistons."

Anger clouds the judgment and hinders concentration. By teaching his players to stay composed emotionally in the face of a physical confrontation, Jackson ensured that attempts to rattle the Bulls with violent shoving, elbowing, or punching failed to produce the desired results.

This level of control is not easy to reach. It can only be achieved if we are aware of the changes going on inside ourselves. As the biofeedback axiom goes, control follows awareness.

So the question is, if control follows awareness, how do we reach this awareness? First, we must see killer instinct in a light unobscured by any moralistic or idealistic shade. We need to realize it is not something to be feared, something to be ashamed of, or something to be carefully hidden away within the deepest part of our minds. Killer instinct is present in each and every one of us. The dilemma, then, becomes what to do with it. In some people, it needs to be tamed or suppressed to a degree; others need to bring it out more. To turn it on or off at will is an incredibly valuable asset, which can only be achieved by proper training and self-knowledge.

"Any situation that causes your blood to boil or your heart to beat a little faster is an opportunity for training."

Awareness is being cognizant of the mental, spiritual, emotional and physiological ramification of the moment. Awareness is being in tune with your surroundings, sensing your effect on them as well as their effect on you. It is not making a judgment call on your observations. For example, if someone cuts you off in traffic and fails to signal an apology, and you experience an overwhelming urge to separate this person's head from his body, you don't instantly clamp down and suppress this urge while berating yourself for your Neanderthal behavior. You simply acknowledge what you are feeling at the moment, what caused you to feel this way, and how you can use this knowledge to your benefit should a real situation arise. Awareness can be cultivated in many ways. Specifically, right now, we are only concerned with awareness in one's self, but the attributes necessary for street awareness can certainly be useful here. However, the catch is that we are dealing with something intrinsically more difficult. We come from a culture of distraction. Television, radio, video games, and endless juicy tabloids serve to distract us from dealing with our seemingly mundane lives. By divorcing our-

"The killer instinct is not a sledge-hammer but a scalpel that must be continually honed."

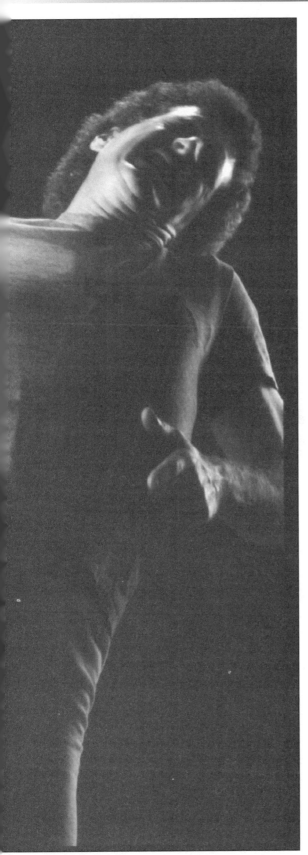

selves from reality, if only for a moment, we lose touch with the one thing that determines our potential for accomplishment — ourselves. How many hours have you spent by yourself, free from any sort of distraction — even hunting or backpacking? I mean time spent walking or sitting, listening only to your body. This is no easy task. Sitting quietly for 20 minutes a day for a week will tell you volumes about yourself. You will find all kinds of intense emotions surfacing for no apparent reason. Your mind will concoct very persuasive arguments against this course of action. This will not be a pleasant experience. Now, I am not espousing any religious and/or spiritual doctrines for this practice. This is simply an exercise to cultivate awareness, because if you can't listen to your body sitting still, you aren't going to hear a thing when Gunnery Sergeant Pat Bagley is drilling uppercuts into your ribs!

Let's say you heeded my advice and now have a working level of awareness. Here's where we get to work on the control aspect. (This is actually the easier part.) Now that you are aware of the changes going on in your body, you should simply try to effect gradual control over these changes. The more acute your awareness, the more successful your attempts will be. Any situation that causes your blood to boil or your heart to beat a little faster is an opportunity for training. It could be a fight with your mate, a particularly condescending teller at the bank, or a check that was supposed to be in the mail. Anything that gets you going is fair game. Instead of flying off the handle, causing considerable damage to your home and furnishings, or suppressing the powerful emotions at play (thereby causing you an ulcer), take a few deep breaths and acknowledge what's happening in your body. You may still be angry, but now it is a controlled anger, which provides eminently usable energy. Make no mistake: Anybody can throw a temper tantrum. Losing your cool is not a sign of strength, but lack of control.

A lot of this may seem obscure, but it really isn't. Think of any great sports figure and pay attention to how he thrives under pressure. He feels the emotions as strongly as the next man, but he knows how to channel and not be overwhelmed by them. Try to recall any accidental killing where the husband or wife took the life of his or her beloved spouse. Through all their regret and grief, one thing is clear — they lost control and didn't realize what they were doing until it was too late. As martial artists we must always be aware of our actions. Not only for the safety of others, but more because we can then act appropriately, decisively, and ruthlessly when the need arises to defend our loved ones or ourselves.

"Killer instinct will allow us to prevail in an ear-biting, eye-gouging streetfight."

The killer instinct is not a sledgehammer but a scalpel that must be continually honed. Killer instinct will allow us to prevail in an ear-biting, eye-gouging streetfight. It is the savvy that clues us into our adversary's weakness. It is the ruthlessness that drives you to mercilessly capitalize on that weakness. It is the impetus that turns your training into fighting. This topic should not be taken lightly; if you intend to be a fighter, you should implement killer instinct development into your training. I have given you one way to train killer instinct. It is perhaps the most beneficial, but also the most frustrating way. The physical logistics of integrating these concepts into your art is up to you, but they must be grounded in these immutable principles. In a crisis, you will not rise to your expectations, but fall to your level of training. Don't let ignorance of killer instinct be your downfall.

Paul squares off with his opponent (1). Opponent jabs, Paul parries (2). Opponent follows with a rear hook (3). Paul does a bob and weave (4). Paul throws an uppercut to opponent's midsection (5) and follows with an overhand to the face (6).

FILIPINO PANANTUKAN (BOXING) DRILLS.

Ready stance with opponent Robert Kincaid (1). Paul parries opponent's jab with his rear hand (2). Opponent throws a right hook (3), which Paul avoids with a bob and weave (4). Paul steps in (5) to throw an overhand hook to his opponent's face (6). He then lands a right uppercut to the stomach (7).

From a ready stance (1) the opponent jabs (2). Paul deflects and moves slightly inside (3). Paul rakes an upward elbow across the deltoid (4), then follows with a rear downward elbow across the opponent's temple (5). He finishes with a knee to the opponent's head (6).

From a ready stance (1) the opponent throws a right jab (2). Paul deflects the jab and rakes his elbow upward across the opponent's bicep (3). Paul follows with a downward elbow to the opponent's deltoid (shoulder) muscle (4).

From a ready stance (1) the opponent throws a low side kick. Paul raises his knee to counter (2) and follows with a thigh kick (3).

Paul squares off with his opponent (1) who prepares to do a spinning kick (2). Paul counters before the kick is launched by raising his foot and delivering a kick to the opponent's back (3).

From a ready position (1), the opponent prepares a side kick (2). Paul counters the kick by driving his elbow into the opponent's leg (3).

From a ready stance (1), the opponent attempts to throw a high side kick (2). Paul pulls back slightly and delivers a shot to the groin (3).

CHAPTER 4

The Filipino Art of Kino Mutai

As we look back on the history of the Philippines, we see much war and bloodshed. During many of the battles the Filipinos were forced to wage, they found themselves outnumbered and outgunned. Imagine having to fight trained Samurai warriors using only farming equipment! Consequently, their ideology was to find a way to put them on equal footing with their adversaries. They were forced to be incredibly innovative when dealing with the harsh reality of the times.

When we use the word "circumvent" we are actually saying, "Find a way to cheat." In the world of weapons, the Filipinos developed an amazing way of "cheating." Instead of blocking strikes, they would actually smash the opponent's weapon hand. By way of analogy, if the opponent were a snake and the weapon was the fang, this method was called "defanging the snake." While the rest of the world would go toe-to-toe weapons fighting, blocking strikes and trading blows, the Filipinos would simply and directly smash the hand.

They used the same ideology with when fighting with empty hands. Instead of blocking punches and kicks, they used nerve destructions against the incoming blows. Instead of trading punches and kicks with their opponents, they would get inside and implement their knees, elbows, and headbutts. Now that we are beginning to understand the central theme of the Filipino paradigm (David overcoming Goliath), let us delve into the world of grappling, and into the topic of this chapter — kino mutai. The term kino mutai literally means "the art of pinching and biting." In jeet kune do we refer to it as "biting and eye gouging," because we prefer to pinch the eyeball. Many Filipino escrimadores possessed an invaluable attribute that most people simply do not have: incredible grip strength. This was a byproduct of wielding heavy sticks, swords, and knives all day. One of the most famous Filipino grandmasters, Floro Villabrille, could actually husk coconuts with his bare hands. This grip strength, combined with biting, is the Filipino way of "cheating" when it comes to grappling. By no coincidence, Bruce Lee also possessed incredible grip strength. He used a lot of innovative equipment to develop that tendon strength in the fingers and forearms.

When discussing eye gouging and biting, the first thing people say is, "Well, anyone can bite!" This bland assertion is true — anyone can bite. But the difference between just plain biting and kino mutai is how to bite, where to bite, and when to bite. When a kino mutai practitioner bites you, it is with an uninterrupted bite. This means he knows the exact

"Find a way to cheat."

places on the body to bite, and with precise timing. He grabs you with his incredible grip strength and bites in areas that would take literally minutes to disengage. There are over 140 areas on the human body that a kino mutai proponent can bite you and hang on for as long as he desires. While he is biting, he is implementing his knowledge of kinesiology along with the attributes of sensitivity and grip strength to hang on like a pit bull.

In the world of wrestling, Brazilian jiu-jitsu practitioners are clearly the kings. Their subtle body movements, ground sensitivity, knowledge of leverage, escapes and finishing moves are in a league of their own. Combining the art of Brazilian jiu-jitsu with the Filipino art of kino mutai creates a hybrid grappling art that is perhaps the most formidable on the planet. Kino mutai allows us to circumvent the jiu-jitsu game. You could rely on kino mutai in a streetfight against a bigger, stronger groundfighter to either beat him on the ground or create enough space to get back to your feet (even if your only goal is to run). When there are no rules, weight classes, or referees, "cheating" may be the only way to survive.

TRAINING METHODS OF KINO MUTAI

HOW TO BITE

In training in kino mutai, we must first ascertain the essential principles and then work each individually. We will first focus on how to bite. A kino mutai practitioner is always cognizant of how much flesh is in his mouth. The average person who doesn't know how to bite properly will try to use all his teeth and take too much "meat" in one bite. Conversely, a kino mutai person will angle his face so the pressure is applied directly on the incisors. The actual motion of the bite is a repeated circular ripping of the flesh, which results in numerous smaller bites. When applied cumulatively, unimaginable damage is inflicted.

The best way to practice this technique is to get a large piece of beef roast and put it inside a t-shirt. Next, get a timer and explode into your bite. The goal is to tear through the entire piece of beef as quickly as possible. In the beginning of this drill, you will encounter several hurdles. First, you will notice your teeth hydroplaning across the surface of the meat without actually penetrating. Varying the angle and pressure of the actual bite (using the attribute of sensitivity) can mitigate this problem. Secondly, halfway through the practice session most people discover one side of their jaw muscle suffering a terrible cramp. When this happens, roll the face to engage the incisors on the opposite side.

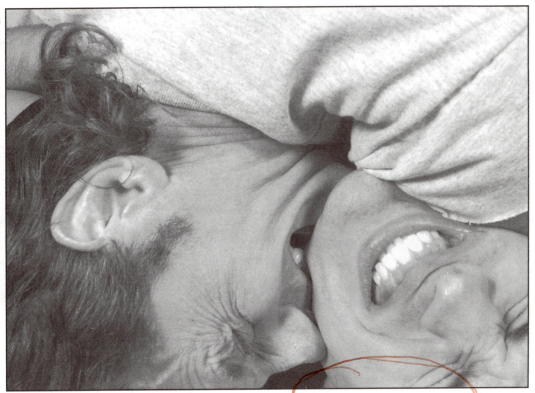

This sequence illustrates the art of Kino Mutai — Filipino biting and eye gouging. The face and neck are very sensitive areas, making them effective targets for biting.

The more times you practice this drill and the better your body mechanics become at tearing (small circular bites), the faster you will be able to gnaw through the beef. In the beginning, it may take you two or three minutes to get through the meat. After 20 or 30 pot roasts (and many barbecues!), you will find you can tear your way through the average five-pound slab of meat inside seconds.

The next point is the single most-important concept of kino mutai: biting someone "uninterrupted." To help define uninterrupted biting, picture having your opponent in a bear hug with your arms wrapped around his torso; or imagine the opponent in your guard, and your arms in a vice grip around his neck while biting his throat. If you do not have a firm grip on the opponent while biting, his visceral response will be to simply pull away. The result will be a small puncture on the opponent that will hardly do the damage that we require. Applying this vice grip while making the small tears with the incisors gives us the ability to hang on and bite the assailant until next leap year!

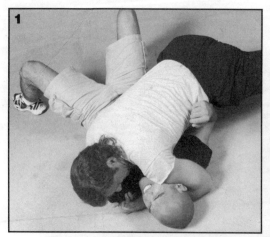

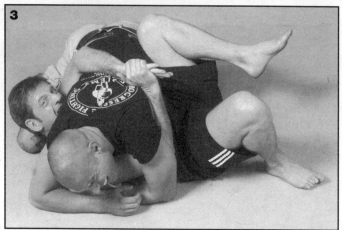

Paul is trapped under his opponent (1), who is mounted in a cross-side position. Paul uses his left knee and his arm to control the opponent (2), then wraps his arms around his opponent's body to secure him in position for an uninterrupted bite (3). Paul begins the bite on the opponent's latissimus muscle of the upper back (4). His opponent attempts to pull away (5). When Paul feels there is enough space between him and his opponent, he pulls his legs in and places his feet on the opponent's chest and shoves him away (6-7).

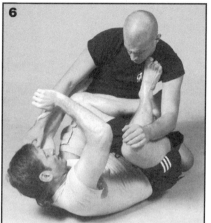

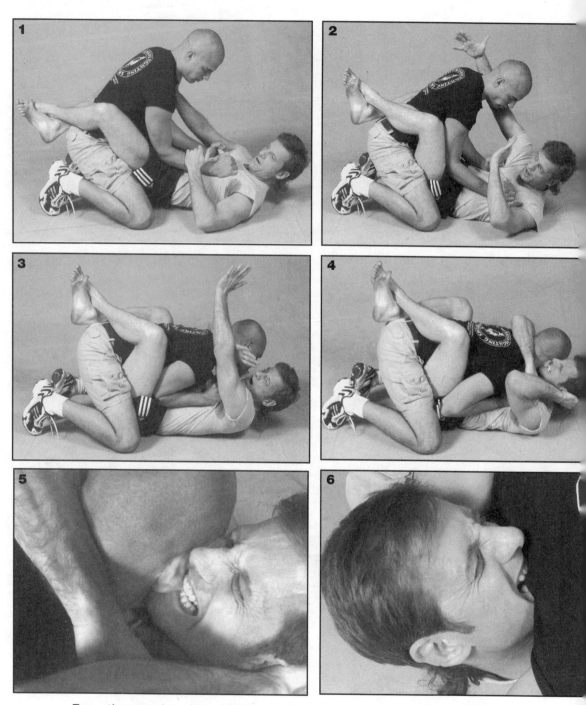

From the guard position (1), Paul pulls his opponent in toward him (2). He secures his opponent in position with his arms (3) and begins the bite on the opponent's ear (4-5) or on the trapezius, which is also a vulnerable area (6).

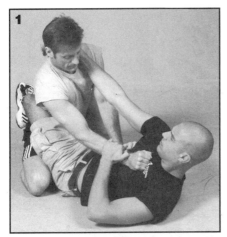

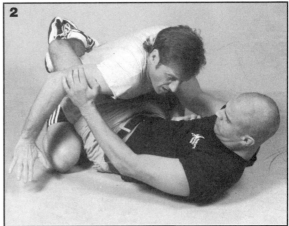

Paul is in his opponent's guard (1). He allows himself to be pulled inward (2). Paul bites the nipple area (3-4), which is quite sensitive to pain.

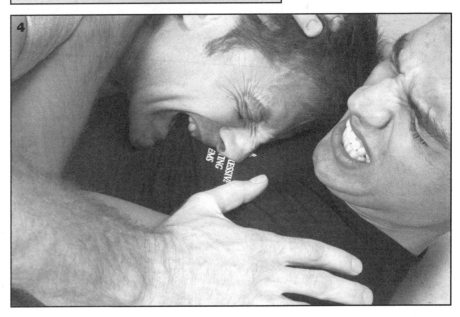

The next sequence illustrates a "street" method of passing the guard — as opposed to the "sport" way. Paul is trapped in his opponent's guard (1). Paul leans forward and delivers a headbutt (2). He then grabs the opponent's biceps to control the arms and avoid being re-grabbed (3). Paul jumps to his feet (4) and delivers several downward strikes to the opponent's groin (5-7).

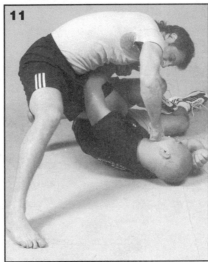

Releasing the opponent's hooks (8), Paul uses his knees to completely escape the legs (9) and quickly pushes the legs to one side (10). He comes to a half-mount position with one knee on the opponent and punches the opponent's face (11).
Paul chambers his right leg to deliver a knee strike to the opponent's temple (12-13).

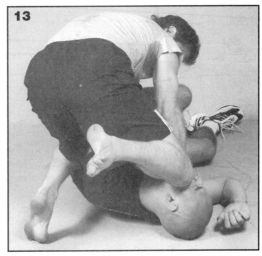

WHERE TO BITE

This brings us to the next principle: where to bite. Yes, you can use your teeth just about anywhere on an opponent's body, but to bite uninterrupted you must target specific areas. What constitutes a "good" area to bite? We have two criteria to determine this:

1. It should be extremely sensitive to pain. The cheek, neck, ear, nipple area, latissimus dorsi (muscle of the back, found just below the armpit), and the groin are all extremely sensitive regions with many nerve endings.

2. It should be an area that allows you to position yourself so your opponent cannot counter your bite by pulling away or pushing you off. The importance of biting a sensitive area while hanging on cannot be overstated. Using some basic positions in jiu-jitsu, we will present just a few of the many possible bites.

a. You are in the top position, mounted: You can bite the face and neck.

b. You are cross-side on your opponent: From here you can bite the cheek, ear or neck.

c. In the north-south position: You have the groin bite.

d. You have the opponent in your guard: Target the cheek, ear, or neck.

e. You are in your opponent's guard: You have the nipple bite.

f. You are on the bottom and your opponent is cross-side: You can bite the lat muscle if his elbow is across your body or his neck if his elbow is elsewhere.

Remember, the key is to hold your opponent so you can bite as long as you want. His visceral response will be to get the source of his pain (your teeth) away from his body as quickly as possible! Thus, he will try to pull away or push you off, depending on your position, which creates space between his body and yours. You then can take advantage of this space and push or kick him off. This is the fastest way to get out from under him if you are pinned underneath someone much stronger and heavier than you. If, however, you fail to hang on to your opponent while you bite, you are not biting uninterrupted. Your opponent will be able to pull away before your bite causes the damage required to get the reaction you need.

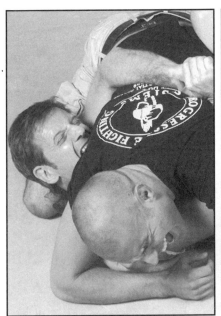

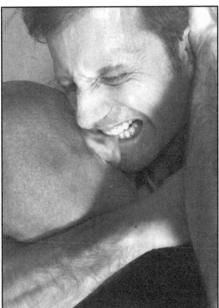

*KINO MUTAI

WHEN TO BITE

Now we come to kino mutai's most-significant training drill. Once you understand the concept of uninterrupted biting, and how to use small circular tears to inflict maximum damage, it's time to institute kino mutai in actual sparring. We have illustrated the basics of how and where to bite; the following drill will help you learn when to bite. Start by rolling on the mat and doing a typical jiu-jitsu practice session. While grappling, begin seeking the appropriate areas of the body to bite (we call this target acquisition). This process could take anywhere from one second-to-five minutes. Timing is critical; only by actually rolling will you develop the proper timing to engage in kino mutai at will. Once you have selected the target area, your next step is to hold your training partner as firmly as you can (grab your own wrist to strengthen the hold). This ensures that your bite will be uninterrupted. Now simulate the bite by pressing your face firmly against the target as long as possible. The moment your training partner feels the vice grip/bite applied, he should instantly attempt any possible defense (e.g., pushing your face away, breaking the hold, etc.). If your technique is applied correctly, it should take your partner at least ten seconds to escape the "bite."

"When you bite someone you cause pain. When you bite uninterrupted so your assailant can't stop what you're doing, you create panic."

The second half of our kino mutai equation is the (uninterrupted) eye gouge. To train the eye gouge use the exact same methodology — first wrestle slowly seeking target acquisition. Each of the positions advantageous for the bite also works well for the eye gouge, with the exception of north-south. Grab your opponent's neck in your vice grip and gently press on the eyeball until your opponent pulls your hand away. As you get better at eye gouging, have your training partner wear swim goggles and practice the eye gouge more aggressively.

One often-overlooked point of kino mutai is the tremendous psychological damage a vicious bite or eye gouge will inflict on attacker. When you bite someone you cause pain. When you bite uninterrupted so your assailant can't stop what you're doing, you create panic. Add to this that you are biting in a sensitive area (both physically and emotionally) and you are in essence destroying him emotionally — completely demoralizing him.

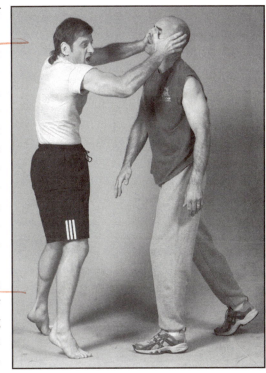

Using kino mutai is an absolute last resort. In this day and age, the thought of having somebody's blood in your mouth is certainly objectionable. However, in a life-or-death situation — perhaps in an alley while pinned on the ground — implementing a bite at a propitious time could be what creates enough space to shed an attacker, get to your feet, and escape. There must be a clear distinction in the martial arts between self-preservation (doing whatever it takes to save yourself and your loved ones) and self-perfection (the sport and training of martial arts). When we think about bludgeoning somebody with a stick, stabbing him with a knife, or biting a hole in someone's face, the subject is quite distasteful (pardon the pun). However, when protecting yourself or the lives of your loved ones, a simple question begs just one answer: Is there anything you wouldn't do?

CHAPTER 5

Edged Weapons Defense

Never has so much been said and written about a subject of which people know so little. Of all the possible topics an instructor could choose (whether unintentionally or not) in which to misinform students, defense against the knife is by far the most dangerous. Anyone claiming to be an expert with a knife who teaches blocking, empty-hand disarms, and low horse stances might as well be teaching students to catch bullets in their teeth.

Because there are so few knifefighting tournaments in the United States, it is difficult for a prospective student to gauge the authenticity of an edged weapons instructor. It seems all one needs to fool the general public is a pair of green army pants, a photo of the instructor with a nasty expression on his face, his knife positioned on his opponent's throat, and SHAZAM! We have "Instant Rambo!"

"SHAZAM! We have instant Rambo!"

By far, the most realistic methods for fighting and training with all types of edged weapons come from the Philippines. Real confrontations with blades are all too common there; their fighting techniques have nothing to do with phony heroism and everything to do with survival. What I would like to do is delineate and prioritize a few of their techniques and training methods.

(1) **FOOTWORK:** Proper footwork is vital to knifefighting; in fact, it is the infrastructure for almost everything we do. Footwork allows us to maintain the correct distance between our opponent and ourselves. Having a low stance with no footwork in this arena is like having a Ferrari with no wheels. We need to move quickly toward, or away from, our opponent. When an attacker has a knife, the necessity for good footwork is tripled.

But what is the proper footwork? When we think of good footwork in the realm of boxing, almost instantly we picture Muhammad Ali or Sugar Ray Leonard. The way these boxers move — light, catlike, sticking and moving — is real knifefighting footwork! When you have a razor-sharp knife in your hand, it is fairly obvious that you do not need to plant your feet to do damage to your opponent. Of course, if you are punching and kicking, it behooves you to get lower and load up for delivering combinations. However, in a knifefight it is far more important to stay as light and as agile as possible. One razor slice across the knifehand or one quick thrust directly in the face may be all it takes to end the altercation. So remember, when a knife is in the hand, get up on your toes and move.

(2) **DISTANCING:** The distance at which we choose to fight our opponent is one of the most important points relative to winning the altercation. In almost every article, video, or seminar I have seen, the instructor has his students knifefighting in boxing range; that is, close enough for the students to exchange punches. Please, watch just one round of your favorite boxing match (any one will do) and count how many times each fighter is hit. Now, imagine if these boxers removed their gloves and had straight razors put into their hands...they would be wallowing in a pool of blood within ten seconds.

There are literally hundreds of drills that involve close-quarter knife and stickwork; however, these drills were developed to improve one's attributes, such as sensitivity, coordination and body mechanics. We call this self-perfection. This should not be confused with real weapons fighting for self-preservation. This is why in real combat, experienced knife-fighters always fight out of what is called largo mano range (just outside of kicking range). The reason is twofold: first, with proper distance he can more easily avoid being sliced, and secondly, his primary objective is cutting his opponent's knife hand, which is also called...

(3) DE-FANGING THE SNAKE: If you can cut the opponent's hand there will be an instant disarm. It is a physical impossibility to hold a knife when the tendons, muscles, and ligaments responsible for movement of the hand are severed. Once you have de-fanged the snake, the snake is harmless and you are now given the choice to kill it or let it go. Using both correct footwork and maintaining the proper distance from an opponent are crucial to de-fanging the snake.

> "Once you have de-fanged the snake, the snake is harmless and you are now given the choice to kill it or let it go."

This same principle also applies to stickfighting. In most modern-day stick tournaments, we see protective headgear on the fighters who are mostly head-hunting. Putting on a helmet and going all-out teaches students how to deal with adrenaline and is certainly a worthwhile experience. This type of practice should constitute about five percent of your training. Also remember to wear protection on the hands, and don't ignore the hand smash! In a tournament, we can witness up to 20 hand smashes without a single point being awarded; yet, when contact to the head is made, points are given. This is simply unrealistic. Generally in stick tournaments, the participants use rattan sticks. The rattan sticks have air going through them; they are considered practice weapons. If stickfighters used no protection for their hands (as in a real fight) and were using real pieces of oval or hexagonal oak or other hardwood, or perhaps using real pieces of lead pipe, any of those neglected hand smashes would shatter every bone in the opponent's hand! Although from a sport viewpoint these types of matches are very entertaining, compared to real combat they are akin to having a pillow fight.

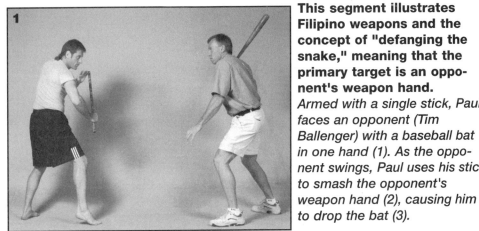

This segment illustrates Filipino weapons and the concept of "defanging the snake," meaning that the primary target is an opponent's weapon hand.

Armed with a single stick, Paul faces an opponent (Tim Ballenger) with a baseball bat in one hand (1). As the opponent swings, Paul uses his stick to smash the opponent's weapon hand (2), causing him to drop the bat (3).

SINGLE STICK VS. SINGLE STICK

Opponent (Steve Blatus) strikes with an angle 1 (high forehand) attack. Paul smashes his hand (1-2). Paul again smashes the opponent's weapon hand as he attacks with a high backhand (3).

The same principle is used to defend against an (low forehand) angle 3 (4) and an angle 4 (low backhand) attack (5). Against a thrust (angle 5), Paul uses body mechanics to avoid the strike while smashing the opponent's weapon hand (6).

**THE FILIPINO MARTIAL ARTS CONCEPT OF DEFANGING
THE SNAKE ILLUSTRATED WITH DOUBLE STICKS.**
*Paul smashes the opponent's hand as he attacks with a high fore-
hand (1). The opponent attacks with the opposite hand (2) and Paul
again smashes the weapon hand.*

Paul's defense doesn't change when facing an opponent with double sticks. Paul continues to attack the weapon hand (3-4).

SINIWALI (DOUBLE STICK) COORDINATION DRILL.
Ready stance (1). Paul and Steve swing a high forehand (2), low backhand (3) and a high backhand (4).

(4) **TIMING:** A sense of timing is equally as important as the attributes of footwork and distancing, although it is certainly more ambiguous and difficult to explain. Timing can be thought of as hitting your opponent either before, during, or after he takes a shot at you. Timing is much more of a "heady" game; you must feel that split-second opening for your shot. When one has an expert sense of timing, he can literally move at one-tenth speed and still connect. I have been hit ten-to-one by old Filipino guys in their 70s. To develop impeccable timing, one needs awareness and line familiarization. These are attributes which tend to improve with age and experience. After sparring briefly with Cocoy Canete, who at age 65 basically used my body for target practice, I asked him (while rubbing my welts) at what age was he in his prime. His response was, "In about another ten or 15 years!" Now let's talk about the relatively less-important points of knifefighting.

1. What is the best way to hold the knife?

In your hand. I have actually seen entire books written on the "proper way" to hold a knife. All that time spent on exactly where your index finger should be placed is time that could (and should) be spent developing functional attributes!

2. What is the best type of knife to carry?

A sharp one!

3. What size knife should I have?

Pardon the cliché, but "It's not the size that counts, it's how you use it!"

As with most things in life, perception is everything. If you perceive the three points mentioned earlier to be the most important points in knifefighting, you will be concentrating on the finger and missing "all the Heavenly glory" (to paraphrase Bruce Lee).

So, what should you do if you are actually attacked by someone with a knife? First, try to run like #@**_%! It has been said that to defend yourself against the blade, you must first learn to fight with the blade. The more you understand the concepts behind fighting with a knife, the more you respect the awesome damage it can inflict. Unlike a punch or a kick, all the blade has to do is make contact. The attacker does not even have to be particularly skilled with a knife to seriously hurt you!

"Unlike a punch or a kick, all the blade has to do is make contact."

Instructors who teach disarming an angry person with a razor are living in a fantasy world. They do not understand the grim reality of a knifefight, most likely because they haven't experienced one. However fun or romantic it may be to picture yourself instantly disarming a knife from a mugger's hand, the reality is that if you were to make such a decision, it could be your very last.

A very simple acid test demonstrates what will not work: Go to the store and buy an industrial-strength, extra-large red marker. Find a confined area and instruct a friend to assault you full speed as though the marker were a live blade (not "locking out" any strikes, just slicing and thrusting quickly). Now, try to apply any blocking or disarming techniques. You will find that you will finish this drill with red lines slashed all over your body! This graphic illustration will hopefully persuade you that running remains the best option.

"The attacker does not even have to be particularly skilled with a knife to seriously hurt you!"

But suppose there is no avenue of escape. Perhaps you are in a crowded restaurant with your family or in a fenced-in area. Option two is for you to find an equalizer. A good first reaction would be to grab a knife if you happen to have one; or you could pick up a bottle to hold the attacker at bay. Projectile weapons are great equalizers — pool balls, a chair, a table, pool cues, hot soup in the guy's face — anything to distract this person so you can safely escape.

Finally, we must discuss one final possibility: You are confronted by an angry person with a razor, there is nowhere to run, and there are no equalizers available. (You are in a handball court with Freddie Krueger guarding the exit!) Personally, I would probably try my odds with a very low and well-timed double-leg takedown, then smother the attacker and simultaneously engage in kina mutai. Even though this strategy may be the most viable, the reality is that I will still be cut by the knife, perhaps fatally.

"My response of choice when confronted by a blade is to run!"

Again, my response of choice when confronted by a blade is to run!

There are many reasons to develop your skill as a knifefighter. Training with a blade is one of the best ways to improve many of the attributes that help you as a martial artist. In terms of self-preservation in an edged weapon attack, you should concentrate your training on the four most important points of knifefighting:

1. FOOTWORK — Light, loose, and up on your toes (like a boxer).

2. DISTANCE — Largo mano range (past kicking range).

3. DE-FANGING THE SNAKE — Make the opponent's knifehand your primary target.

4. TIMING — Flight time, flight time, and more flight time!

CHAPTER 6

Jeet Kune Do and Police Use of Force

By Larkin Fourkiller and Michael Holsapple

INTRODUCTION

Police officers worldwide know all too well the dangers and risks associated with law enforcement. Every 57 hours an American police officer is killed in the line of duty. Today's peace officers must police a special population, including some prone to weapon usage, violent gang and drug activities, mandatory prison sentences, hate factions, and the ever-present sector of society's drunk, drugged, deranged, and career criminals, many of whom exhibit little regard for authority.

Law enforcement officers are constantly subjected to the unpredictable and violent side of human behavior, where at any given moment they can find themselves in a life-threatening situation. With nearly 300 officers killed in the last two years, the police profession needs to be ever vigilant in its efforts to protect the protector. Therefore, police officers should receive the necessary training to help them survive violent altercations. Is this the case now? Could some police deaths and injuries be prevented?

THE TRAINING DILEMMA

Contemporary policing practices have often mandated officers to fulfill a role of specialization rather then their traditional tasks as a generalist. Modern law enforcement agency personnel are not only required to deal with the "routine" complaints we accept as commonplace, but now must be responsive to a host of technological issues, public expectations, a drug war, and an ever-increasing number of calls for service.

Some of these demands and priorities include forensics and specialized investigative efforts, drug interdiction enforcement, school safety and juvenile prevention/intervention strategies, policing of the Internet, increased participation in community forums, special operations missions (SWAT and drug enforcement support), and tasks associated with community policing programs.

Associated with these undertakings are (1) commitment of personnel; (2) fiscal considerations; (3) specialized training needs; and (4) time-management issues. For some agencies these new specialized roles and responsibilities only serve to compound administrative attempts at providing the basic or in-service training wanted and needed by their officers.

PERCEPTION VS. REALITY

Anytime the police are required to use some type of force there are often repercussions. No doubt violence is an ugly thing, but those who are called upon to deal with such chaos and hostilities are the police. It is their duty to intervene wherever and whenever violence occurs, and in doing so they are sometimes required to use force to protect themselves and others.

It seems there often is a misguided perception that the police could and should resolve each of these dangerous incidents without violence or injury. This "officer-friendly" expectation is like asking officers to play "touch" in a "tackle" football game. It is important we be reminded that perception is not reality.

Reality can be deadly. Despite the possibility of citizen complaints, threats of civil action, and an ironic predisposition of American police to cater to perceptions, police officers need the skills to survive violent hand-to-hand confrontations.

> "Many officers are reluctant to use force — even deadly force, to defend themselves, though circumstances clearly justify its use."

Many officers are reluctant to use force — even deadly force, to defend themselves, though circumstances clearly justify its use.

Fear of disciplinary action and civil liability, lack of public, political, and departmental support, and pressure from special interest groups can all be contributing factors in not only the way police protect (or fail to protect) themselves, but just as importantly, the training (or inadequate training) officers receive.

For some police officers, such unfavorable attention can often (both consciously or unconsciously) override the appropriate response even when their personal safety is at risk. As a result, when an officer finds himself in a hand-to-hand altercation, he may not only be hesitant to act decisively, but may also lack a viable countermeasure. This hesitation can cause him to miss a "window of opportunity" to end the confrontation (allowing it instead to escalate beyond his control).

TRADITIONAL POLICE USE OF FORCE TRAINING

To fully appreciate the role of jeet kune do in future police training, one needs to be know where law enforcement use of force training was and is today.

Over the years policing has traveled from one extreme to the other in terms of personnel, technology, and attitude. Years ago, there was a two-prong test potential police applicants had to pass. Those special requirements were — being big and tough. With those physical attributes – along with a badge, gun, nightstick, and common sense — an officer was expected to ensure peace and tranquility on his beat.

USE OF FORCE CONTINUUM

One positive aspect of modern defensive tactics training is the conception and utilization of the police use of force continuum. This framework delineates various types of suspect resistance and correlates the coinciding appropriate police response. This instrument serves as a helpful guide in understanding the relationship between that resistance which is demonstrated by the offender and the type of control attempted by the police to counter it. Its application is widespread within the law enforcement community, not only serving as a practical teaching aid, but also clarifying departmental policies and procedures. The force continuum also educates the tier of fact within the judicial setting and assists the public in understanding the actions of police in those situations where questions arise concerning force employed by police.

Several different versions of this continuum have been created by training professionals within the police defensive tactics ranks. Although opinions differ in some areas within the framework (justification level for chemical application), the continuum itself usually represents similar schools of thought.

TYPICAL POLICE FORCE CONTINUUM

The force continuum identifies two distinct actions: (1) Resistance offered by the suspect, and (2) Actions used by the police. The actions range from the lowest levels of force (minimal) to the most serious – deadly or lethal force.

Supplementing the force continuum are important officer-subject factors, as well as contributing circumstances which can influence the type of control an officer might use. Some of these factors and special circumstances include: gender, size, skill level, age, number of suspects, exhaustion/injury, reaction time, number of officers, and special knowledge.

TENSE AND EXTRAORDINARY CIRCUMSTANCES

...officers frequently have to make "split-second judgments" concerning the use of force, under "circumstances that are tense, uncertain and rapidly evolving..."
— *Graham v. Conner (1989)*

Police are often cast into scenes of mass confusion and uncooperative attitudes. They must interact with individuals who are suffering from any number of influencing factors: emotional distress; intoxication; prejudices; irrational behavior; and a propensity for showmanship. Throw in other variables, such as subjects with extreme tolerance to pain and unpredictable environmental conditions (bars, glass-covered floors, busy thoroughfares), not to mention an officer's overreliance on equipment and a reluctance to act (discussed earlier), and it is easy to understand Murphy's Law: "Whatever can go wrong — will go wrong."

"Whatever can go wrong – will go wrong."

"It is important to remember that in any police-suspect confrontation there is always at least one weapon present — the officer's gun. Sadly, many officers are injured and killed with or in spite of this force option."
— *Fourkiller*

Weapon malfunction; inability to secure weapons because of being pinned or surprised; being grounded; attacks by multiple suspects; unexpected threats from edged or bludgeon weapons; shooting and missing; injury or exhaustion; unable to deploy discriminate fire; correctional environment (unarmed and outnumbered); off-duty and unarmed; undercover and unarmed; special operations (SWAT); and criminal investigators with limited weaponry make up just some of potentially deadly confrontational scenarios where specialized close-range fighting skills are needed.

The lack of viable countermeasures for just such circumstances demonstrates the limitations of traditional police self-defense programs. When questions arise, either in the training classroom or in the field, pertaining to serious hand-to-hand encounters, officers are often given the ambiguous suggestion, "Do whatever it takes."

POLICE DEFENSIVE TACTICS LIMITATIONS

"Using no way as way, having no form as form."

— *Bruce Lee*

Standard defensive tactics training presently addresses police use of force issues through classroom lecture, firearms qualifications, impact weapons, chemical agent certification, and a basic course in self-defense.

Most officers receive their most intense and comprehensive instruction during a week-long session at the police academy. Most departments may offer periodic (usually once a year) refresher training. A few progressive agencies take a more active approach by integrating reality-based confrontational simulations. However, there is a significant number of departments that provide little or no follow-up training.

Shortcomings commonplace among police organizations relating to defensive tactics programs include: limited techniques; lack of a realistic fighting philosophy; few reality-based training methods; overreliance on a certain style; and an institutionalized resistance to change. This is not only extremely frustrating for departmental trainers who recognize and advocate new methods, but is also extremely hazardous for officers who inadvertently are left with few resources to defend themselves.

Traditional police self-defense programs focus on those techniques and tactics designed to control individuals who offer minimal resistance. Principles such as positioning, balance displacement, jointlocks, pressure points, and verbal persuasion comprise the majority of this instruction.

In most cases this type of control is appropriate, but there are situations where these basic techniques are ineffective and unrealistic. Police officers are frequently placed in violent and dangerous situations, where the threat of physical confrontation is likely to result in serious injury or death. Often outnumbered, occasionally overmatched, and always weapon involved (officer's weapon), many officers find themselves ill-prepared to deal with these types of violent "street-fights" to the finish. Here is a case in point.

Since 1990 more than 84,000 police officers have been battered and/or injured, and nearly 800 killed during felonious assaults. More than half were shot within five feet of their assailant.

"Police officers are frequently placed in violent and dangerous situations where these basic techniques are ineffective and unrealistic."

In January, 1991, East Texas police Constable Darrell Lunsford made a traffic stop during which he was overpowered, taken to the ground, and killed with his own gun. Just after his discovery of drugs and despite his 6-foot-7, 300-pound frame, he was overwhelmed by three suspects who attacked simultaneously. His murder was captured on his in-car video camera and the recording has since been viewed by thousands of officers to prevent similar tragedies.

This type of critical incident proves the need for improved specialized close-range fighting skills among today's law enforcement professionals.

JEET KUNE DO AND POLICE OFFICER SURVIVAL

Although the ingredients (various martial arts) of the jeet kune do "cocktail" are well-established, its application to law enforcement and the police tactical community is cutting-edge. Anyone who has examined its teachings would immediately appreciate its applicability within the police use of force arena.

Jeet kune do's effective and efficient fighting system meets the police defensive tactics training and operational goals and objectives. Some of those standards are: training must be reality-based; methods must be easily learned and retained; techniques must work; applications must coincide with the force continuum; not dependent upon size or strength; applicable to a wide range of operational needs; and contain a reality-based fighting philosophy.

From a physical and technical perspective, jeet kune do provides officers with a host of techniques and tactics that have applicability throughout the various levels of the police force continuum.

The recognition that more intense types of empty-hand force control may be needed to overcome a combative suspect is just one of the reasons why jeet kune do should be considered preeminent within the law enforcement profession.

The police culture, like many other groups, likes to have its cake and eat it too. Public officials and police administrators tout a zero-tolerance agenda and pontificate aggressive police enforcement to combat crime. Such directives often require officers to become even more involved, and exposed to, the violence that is the mainstay of criminal activity.

It would stand to reason that these same officers would be involved in a higher number of use-of-force incidents. A proficiency in self-defense would be paramount to their safety, which brings us back to training.

Police officers need a variety of methods for controlling uncooperative suspects, including specialized empty-hand skills to survive life-threatening encounters at close-range — the latter a consideration which has been virtually non-existent in a number of police training programs. Jeet

kune do's concepts and philosophies include a variety of fighting styles that fill in gaps which currently exist in some police defensive tactics programs. Stand-up (close-quarter), ground, biting, and knifefighting techniques, as well the tactical ability to flow from one fight forum to another, are just some of the important aspects relevant to police use of force.

STAND-UP (CLOSE-QUARTER)

The Rapid Assault Tactics (RAT) program teaches officers to fight in trapping range (close quarters). Learning how to properly utilize the body's most devastating personal tools — headbutts, knees, and elbows — helps an officer quickly neutralize a serious threat before it can escalate beyond control. As noted earlier, more than half the deadly force encounters occur within five feet.

Police recognition and incorporation of these Level III fight-ending techniques and tactics can help an embattled officer overcome an attacker's attempt to overpower him. An officer would be remiss to think that incapacitation would not follow efforts to ground or subdue him.

Other components of the RAT system are useful to police and are appropriate throughout the parameters of acceptable control efforts used by police. For instance, nerve destructions (Level II) are an effective counter against kicks and punches.

Scene management requires an officer to focus attention on several activities contemporaneously (victims, suspects, witnesses, radio traffic, etc.), which give him little time to react to personal threats, such as a jab or kick. Nerve destruction tactics utilize economy of motion and facilitate a quicker response.

Often times the officer will already have his hands up (safety precaution, hand gestures accompanying verbal directions, such as "calm down and/or move back." A quick lift of the elbow or knee helps an officer intercept an incoming blow and cause extreme pain and distraction. This can be followed up with whatever response (headbutt, thigh kick, jointlock) the circumstance dictates.

Completing the RAT program are those Level I techniques which counter the most-common type of force used by uncooperative suspects: minimal resistance. Here, the use of dumog and tai chi (arts to move the body), along with the application of various jointlocks, appropriately supplement those controlling systems already used by police. Dumog not only is effective in moving uncooperative individuals from point A to point B, but if needed, it can instantaneously facilitate a takedown or a segue into a more serious tactic (headbutt, knee, elbow) should the situation deteriorate into a more risk-prone encounter.

GROUNDFIGHTING

An obvious venue of hand-to-hand combat is the ground. Training for this possibility has been largely ignored despite the knowledge that many situations will ultimately go to the ground. The popularity of "tough-man contests" and the success of grapplers in such events produced a hunger within the defensive tactics community for tactical groundfighting, with Brazilian jiu-jitsu being the most prevalent. This long, overdue aspect of defensive tactics fortunately has been enthusiastically accepted among police trainers and agencies.

The benefit of defending oneself should the fight go horizontal has been made readily apparent throughout this text. Knowing basic grappling countermeasures, augmented with kina mutai and Level III techniques, will undoubtedly leave a grounded officer in a far more advantageous posture.

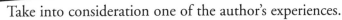

Interwoven among the technical aspects of these martial arts are fighting tenets which clarify objectives and underscore the overall survival doctrine of jeet kune do. Bruce Lee addressed one such doctrine this way: "Where there is a way, therein lies the limitation."

Take into consideration one of the author's experiences.

During a training assignment with an elite military team, three of its members asked Paul and his friend to accompany them on an extracurricular night operation. Paul's first impression was right — 20-plus motorcycles out front equated to a traditional tough biker bar. Paul's hosts were not only huge but had a passion for groundfighting. Paul's friend, besides being a martial artist, was also a pool shark, and it was during one of his many table runs that hostilities began to erupt. And when they finally did, although severely outnumbered (20-5), Paul's team had the three biggest players, and at that point he thought, a fighting chance. That was until the melee began, and as Paul so adamantly stated, "Do you know what those three huge groundfighters did? That's right, each of them took one guy to the ground, leaving the two of us with...well you can do the math."

Besides being just a little angry and requiring hospitalization, Paul's real-life experience helps illustrate the limitations of relying on any one fight-survival discipline.

Too many negative factors are present in the real world of policing to advocate a preference for the ground. Environmental conditions and tactical considerations, such as ground surface (for sure it will not be a mat),

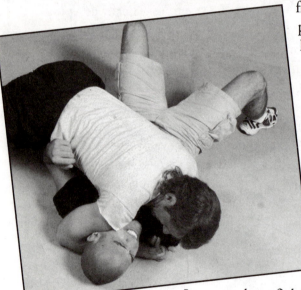

fight location, number of suspects, unpredictability of the landing, cumbersome burden of duty gear, and the difficulty in protecting your weapon, are just a few. In addition, physical affects (exhaustion/injury) and unrealistic applications (on the street you at some point have to relinquish a jointlock) are just a few reasons for not going to the ground. And if grounded, the primary objective is simple — to get up.

In a stand-up fighting position an officer has a better opportunity to employ a firearm, zoning tactics, impact weapons, chemical agents, and his most effective personal weapons — headbutts, knees, and elbows.

Unless it's a sporting event — and police-suspect altercations are not — there are just far too many extenuating factors to prefer this forum. Going to the ground jeopardizes yourself, your partner, or your family in some circumstances. Many fights go to the ground; exposing officers to grappling techniques is an extremely important component in any defensive tactics program.

KNIFEFIGHTING

Another area full of inaccurate and tactically challenged teachings involves the arts of knifefighting and stickfighting. Today, there is an increased number of police officers carrying knives both on and off duty. Although edged weapon training is more readily available today, many officers who carry these weapons are virtually unskilled in its technical and tactical applications.

The (false) confidence officers glean from possessing a knife can, in fact, be detrimental in real-life situations. Cutting angles, range considerations, primary target acquisition, distance issues, and (unrealistic) blocking methods constitute some of the required basic tactical knowledge.

Jeet kune do addresses these concerns with simple, but realistic techniques and a practical training methodology which stresses the obvious (but not often taught) preferred strategy of distance — to run or get an equalizer if you must fight. Other lessons focus on objectives at long range (defanging the snake), close range (cut-then-block) and the ever-availability of headbutts, knees, and elbows.

An excellent police training exercise is the "First To The Knife" drill. A knife is thrown near two officers who are participating in a sparring forum. At its (knife) presentation, the officers race to secure it. The officer who realizes he cannot win then turns and runs to gain distance while formulating a countermeasure. The class applauds the action, because it reinforces the tactical necessity of distance and validates a person's decision not to fight when unarmed.

This encouragement is not only needed to help change a cultural (police) conditioning, but also serves to reinforce an important tactical consideration — the 21-foot reactionary gap between an officer and a knife-wielding suspect.

> "The (false) confidence officers glean from possessing a knife can, in fact, be detrimental in real-life situations."

The next sequence illustrates an energy/sensitivity drill with the knife. The drill begins with Paul delivering an overhand thrust with a knife (1). Erin turns her body to evade the knife and blocks it with her forearm (2). Paul attempts to slice the midsection, Erin maintains contact with his knife hand, redirecting the knife away from her body (3).

Erin continues to follow the movement of the knife, maintaining contact with Paul's arm (4). Paul has completed a "U"-shaped slice, ending with a backhand thrust toward Erin's other shoulder. Erin picks up the contact with the other forearm (5). Paul begins the "U" slice in the opposite direction, while Erin attempts to maintain the contact and keep the blade from touching her (6).

From the "U" sensitivity drill (1), Erin inserts an eye jab (2), while redirecting the knife with her other hand (3). From a different point in the drill (4) she can deliver a knee strike to Paul's groin (5).

At an appropriate point in the sensitivity drill (1), Erin redirects Paul's knife downward to free the high line (2) for a headbutt to Paul's face (3).

The next sequence illustrates the concept of "defanging the snake" from the Filipino arts, using edged weapons. Knife vs. knife with opponent Erin Vunak (1). As the opponent strikes with a downward slash (2), Paul steps back to evade and slices opponent's weapon hand (3).

Against a forehand slash to the midsection, Paul parries the weapon hand as he defangs the snake (4). Against a low backhand slash, Paul redirects the weapon with his empty hand while cutting or thrusting to the face (5).

VENUE-TO-VENUE CONCEPT

Becoming aware of the venue-to-venue concept (flowing from one style to the next) is vital in preparing for and surviving physical altercations. Police-suspect engagements do not take place in a controlled setting (ring or mat), and are subject to only one rule (at least for the suspect). That is, there are no rules! Fights go from stand-up, to the ground, back to stand-up, to knives, to guns.

Without training, an officer can quickly find himself out of his element (preferred fighting style), which can result in a loss of focus (panic) and a tendency to mount a limited defense. For some officers this defense consists of just hanging on and praying that back-up quickly arrives quickly.

> **"He went from aggressor to victim – just like that!"**

KINA MUTAI

Kina mutai, the art of biting and eye gouging, is not only a devastating tactic, but also speaks to the psychology of fighting, as illustrated in the infamous Evander Holyfield-Mike Tyson heavyweight championship fight. Holyfield, despite taking a barrage of punches from arguably the world's hardest hitter, continued his relentless pursuit of Tyson around the ring. Then came the bite. Holyfield immediately quit fighting, placed his hands to his injured ear, and began screaming and jumping around the ring. To many sports fans it was a cheap shot, but in the realm of street-fighting, consider its effects. The biting technique not only caused Holyfield to stop fighting, but psychologically took him out of his element (boxing). He went from aggressor to victim — just like that!

CONCLUSION

It should come as no surprise that law enforcement can benefit from the concepts and philosophies of jeet kune do. Bruce Lee's attention and focus on what works and what doesn't in real-life streetfights are exactly what contemporary police trainers are now advocating. That is the concept of reality-based defensive tactics. Jeet kune do's attention to attributes, functionality, simplicity, reliability, and retainable fighting methods parallel the goals of current police tactical ideology.

The demands of their job force police into violent situations where their training, or lack thereof, can mean the difference between life and death. Police are called upon to intervene in dangerous and unpredictable situations. They must confront suspects intent on resisting, assaulting, or killing the officer.

Defensive tactics designed to quell minimal resistance is often times sufficient, but past lessons of violence and tragedy have demonstrated a need for more comprehensive and realistic-type techniques. Preparing officers to respond physically and psychologically to dangerous hand-to-hand encounters will greatly increase their chances of survival.

Bruce Lee's multi-disciplinary approach and emphasis on developing personal attributes, such as speed, timing, line familiarization, leverage, and sensitivity, ensures the functional application from a training to an operational forum.

Jeet kune do is being refined and adapted to fit the needs of the moment. This is in direct contrast to some systems which advocate strict compliance of their methods, products, and terminology. Jeet kune do's refreshing philosophical approach to such rigid conformity was best summed up by the author of this book at his Progressive Fighting System's 1999 Sierra Summit Retreat: "Instead of telling you which path to take or which mountain to climb, jeet kune do gives you the skills to take whichever path you want, and to climb whatever mountain you choose."

Authors: Larkin Fourkiller, M.S.

Police Captain and Special Enforcement Team Commander. FBI National Academy Graduate and Adjunct Faculty Indiana University-Kokomo. Instructor in Defensive Tactics, Civil Disturbance Control, and Less Lethal Weaponry. He has served as a consultant for several departments and has provided technical assistance to police trainers and tactical teams throughout the country. Contact him at L4Killer@email.com

Michael Holsapple, M.S.

Police Captain and Multi-Agency Drug Task Force Commander. FBI National Academy Graduate. State/National Certified Instructor. Adjunct Faculty, Indiana University-Kokomo.

Bibliography

1. Worden, May. APBnews.com. "Honoring the Fallen: 280 Others Remembered." 2000.

2. Law Enforcement Officer Memorial Statistics. 2000. Washington, D.C.

3. National Institute of Justice. FBI Uniform Crime Report (1997)

4. Pepper Spray Evaluation Project. International Association of Chiefs of Police. June, 1995. pg. 58...It is common knowledge that a high percentage of officers who are incapacitated or have had their guns taken away from them are later shot with their own weapons... It would be unconscionable to ask an officer to take a chance that the OC spray attacker is merely going to walk away after incapacitating the officer.

CHAPTER 7

HIV Implications of a Streetfight in the New Millennium

I am frequently asked about the possibility of contracting HIV as a result of a streetfight. This question is usually brought up during the discussion of kina mutai. This is certainly is a logical question when one pictures someone's blood in your mouth.

I first approached this dilemma in 1986. As a result I investigated the issue with some of the world's leading immunologists — among them Dr. Ho (one of the original discoverers of the virus); Dr. David Hardy of the University of California-Los Angeles; and Dr. Michael Gottlieb, a pioneer in HIV research. When I first posed the question to them, they said there were no reported cases of anyone having contracted the virus as a result of a streetfight. Basically, the odds of transmission were unquantifiable.

As the years went on and more and more cases of HIV were reported, more information became available. Doctors had developed tests called the ELISA and the Western Blot, which could not detect the virus itself, but could detect the antibodies that occur when the virus is present in the body. Around the years 1989-1991, during my years with the Navy SEAL teams in Virginia, I saw my share of streetfights. On many occasions I would find myself drenched in blood — both mine and my assailant's. This led me to continue my edification on the possibility of contracting the virus.

It was around this time that two new tests were developed, both more sophisticated in their ability to detect infection by HIV. One was a much more sensitive antibody test called radio immune precipitation assay (or RIPA for short). The other signaled a major breakthrough in AIDS research because it could actually detect the virus itself, not just the antibodies. This test was called a Polymerase Chain Reaction (PCR). This test acts like a copy machine, replicating the virions (virus particles) and detecting extremely minute particles. (AIDS, being a retrovirus, has extremely small virions). Another major advantage of the PCR test is that one can obtain test results in as little as 14 days from the potential date of infection. Previous to the PCR, there was a three-to-six month window for the body to produce enough antibodies to be detectable.

Once doctors could determine the exact viral load (through the PCR), they understood to a much greater degree how the virus was transmitted. Their conclusion was that the most likely scenario for transmission would be for contaminated blood to find its way directly into the bloodstream itself. This is why intravenous drug users are at such a high risk for contracting HIV. In the early 1990s, the Center for Disease Control produced a statistic that only 1 in 220 people (nurses or other medical professionals) who had accidentally pricked themselves with HIV-contaminated needles would actually seroconvert, and subsequently produce antibodies.

Going back to the scenario of contracting HIV by biting someone, you must understand that the mouth is a mucous membrane, and is not a direct portal into the bloodstream (as long as there are no open sores on the mouth.). First, when you bite someone you will not always get blood in your mouth. Secondly, the possibility of any virus particles surviving the digestive acids of the stomach would be extremely unlikely.

This is not to say that it is impossible to contract HIV through a mucous membrane, as there have been a small number of infections reported. However, it is much less likely than if HIV-positive blood goes directly into the bloodstream. A more likely scenario for infections is that we would simply cause our opponent to bleed (through punch, kick, or other strike) and that blood then makes contact with any open wound. These open wounds could literally be microscopic in nature: a fingernail scrape, punctures on the knuckles from hitting teeth, "road rash," etc. If you've ever watched a college or professional basketball game, you may have noticed that any time a player starts bleeding from an injury, officials instantly remove the player from the game. The player is allowed back on the court only after the bleeding has been contained and the wound properly dressed.

"As with anything in life, one should assess the risk-to-reward ratio."

Maybe we should all re-evaluate our paradigm of streetfighting. As with anything in life, one should assess the risk-to-reward ratio. If the potential risk is contracting a deadly disease, then you need to carefully evaluate what the "reward" for fighting would be. If it is to save your life or the lives of your family, then the answer is clear. However, if the reward is ego-based and you're fighting because someone just made an obscene gesture, then the end may not justify the means.

CHAPTER 8

Women's Self-Defense: Escape to Gain Safety

T he time an individual spends in the martial arts (both frequency and duration) depends on his or her motivation. While some find it enough to take a few classes or a seminar, others dedicate their lifetimes to the "way". I frequently encounter people with varied reasons for participation in the arts. This chapter is not geared toward the female martial artist, but rather toward women who may have taken a weekend self-defense or a "rape prevention" course, and left either with a false sense of security or feeling more confusion than confidence.

Many women never intend to dedicate more than the minimum amount of time it takes for them to feel more confident in an attack situation. Questioning them illustrates the overwhelming worry that the majority of women share: "I'm afraid if it were real, I would just freeze up and forget everything!" The words "forget" and "everything" imply they think they have a lot to remember.

Unfortunately, most instructors rarely adapt their art to the average woman. Catering to the particular limitations of these students is essential and requires consideration of the following points:

> 1. Most men often begin martial arts training with the preconceived notion that they will soon be kicking butt and taking names. A woman, however, sees a radically different and more frightening picture. Her mind is on the serious realities of an attack/rape! Others like her are being assaulted every day; knowing this causes her to develop a legitimate worry (not convoluted by the male ego or delusions of grandeur fostered by *Billy Jack* movies).

2. Women have a different morphology, generally speaking, from men. And so they must learn different techniques and principles, which emphasize different qualities (attributes) and use different training methods than the average male martial artist.

3. Finally, most women simply don't put in the same fight time in a self-defense class that a man might in the dojo. He can get away with learning technique upon technique, kata upon kata, addicted to the black belt "carrot" being dangled in front of him.

For these reasons, women who want self-defense will find that the traditional arts' myriad of techniques, usually better suited for a tournament fight than a street attack, simply don't constitute a viable self-defense program. The mentality of "If he does this, then you do that" is ineffective because there are too many things "he" can do! If a specific technique is taught for each possible scenario, the very fear most women express may well come true — they will freeze up and forget everything.

Jeet kune do encompasses aspects that perfectly translate into an effective self-defense approach for women. Two major JKD concepts central to women's self-defense are adaptability and simplicity. Any techniques taught as part of a self-defense program have to be simple; that is, they should be easy to learn, easy to do, and easy to remember. All techniques should also be adaptable; in other words, a technique should work in a variety of situations against a variety of attacks. I developed a program specifically for women and non-martial artists which addresses these specific needs. This program is called "Escape To Gain Safety." It decreases the fear of forgetting a multitude of techniques, while effectively dealing with most attack scenarios.

The way in which a woman is attacked is not of paramount importance in the Escape To Gain Safety program. Rather, the program emphasizes Bruce Lee's concept of attacking the closest target with the longest weapon. A man assaulting a woman rarely (if ever) begins in a stance, jabbing or kicking. Close-quarter scenarios (grabs, pulls, or holds) make up a large part (at least 85 percent) of the attacks being considered.

Now that the woman's attention is placed on striking a target instead of remembering a technique for each possible situation (there could be an infinite number of these), where to hit becomes the all-important question. Virtually every attack exposes effective targets for a solid strike. There are only four targets to be concerned with, one or more of which will always be available: the eyes, throat, groin and shins. These are vulnerable areas on the body, regardless of size, strength, or physical conditioning.

Obviously, the best defense is common sense and preventative steps, such as avoiding high-risk areas whenever possible. Try to steer clear of alleyways, dark streets, and parking lots at night or when alone. Proper psychology can also be very important if avoidance fails, but when it comes down to it, what to say to an assailant can be just as difficult to remember as what to do to him. So, keep it simple.

"The desired outcome is to survive, not overcome an attacker."

Should an attack become physical, a woman's strategy should be simple as well. Too often, women are taught sequences of several follow-up blows. Although it might look good in the gym, this is not recommend. Once the first effective blow is delivered and the attacker is momentarily distracted or stunned, scream and run like hell! When an attacker gets his eyes or throat jabbed, his groin hit, or his shin smashed, it is unlikely he will have quite the same intent to chase her down the street for another try! The desired outcome is to survive, not overcome an attacker.

Now, let's go back to the original (and legitimate) worry plaguing most women: forgetting the techniques. All a woman has to remember is striking, grabbing, or biting one of the four targets. Those targets fit into a convenient acronym:

Escape	To	Gain	Safety
Y	H	R	H
E	R	O	I
S	O	I	N
	A	N	S
	T		

Of course, locating and striking the targets effectively require training, drilling, and a lot of thought and awareness. No approach is guaranteed. However, I do guarantee this: One is less likely to forget everything one has learned if what one learns is less complicated. This concept can benefit not only women, but any martial artist or non-martial artist who wants to feel more confident about his or her own personal safety.

CHAPTER 9

Legal Issues: Self-Defense in the Courtroom

By Bruce Aukerman, Attorney-at-Law

CHAPTER FOREWORD

Since much of this book is about self-preservation, in today's "sue-happy" world this very well may be the most important chapter! Spending three-to-five years in the "Graybar Hotel" for biting a hole in someone's face is not my idea of self-preservation! The legal arena is clearly not my area of expertise, so I will pass the baton to someone who is world-class in it — my close friend, Bruce Aukerman.

Throughout this chapter I will touch upon several subjects, but the main focus will be on the law as it relates to self-defense. At the outset I must tell you though, the law on this subject is as high as it is wide, and does not lend itself to an easy summation. In the United States there are multiple jurisdictions, both state and federal, and many hundreds of court decisions and statutes dealing with your right to protect yourself and your family from harm.

It would be impossible to cover the waterfront of these decisions and statutes in a book, much less in one chapter. The intent of this chapter is twofold. First, to provide you with a very general understanding of the law of self-defense. Secondly, to stimulate within you a desire to take this general understanding to a local public, college or law school library and research the law in the state where you live. If you do so, you will learn, and you will be better for having done it.

In simple terms, self-defense is a legal defense, which may justify the use of force, even deadly force, to save your life or to remain free from harm. It was first recognized as a legal defense by a 1534 English statute. Since then, the legal defense of self-defense has been adopted and implemented throughout Anglo-American jurisprudence, and is asserted in both criminal and civil cases in the United States on a daily basis.

People often ask what they are allowed to do if and when they are attacked on the street, in their home, or on their way to work. I understand their desire for specifics, but as you will see, the law of self-defense is factually dependent. That is, depending on the facts of a given situation, your rights may change. In general terms, when attacked, you and every other law-abiding person have the absolute right to do what is reasonably necessary to stay alive and unharmed. This is man's natural law right. In some cases, if all you must do to stay free from harm is walk away, then that is what should be done, and this is what the law will expect you to do. In other cases, such as when physically attacked by a person intending to do you serious bodily harm, or cause your death, you have the right to fight, and the right to win that fight.

"Under the circumstances, what was reasonable and necessary?"

What prevents anyone, including me, from telling others that "you are allowed by law to do A, B, and C, and follow it up with X, Y, and Z", is that self-defense, in a legal sense, is very dynamic and constantly changing, depending on the facts of each case. What may clearly be a justified use of force by an 85-year-old grandmother may not be justified if done by the heavyweight champion of the world. This is not to say that rights change depending on who you are or what you are. Everyone, including the heavyweight champ, has the right to stay alive and unharmed when faced with an attack, assuming he did not provoke that attack. However, the amount of force it may take to keep the 85-year-old grandmother safe may well be different, perhaps even more deadly, than the amount and type of force necessary to keep the heavyweight champ safe. The key is: Under the circumstances, what was reasonable and necessary?

The statutory law of self-defense in my state (Indiana) is as follows:

A. A person is justified in using reasonable force against another person to protect himself or a third person from what he reasonably believes to be the imminent use of unlawful force. However, a person is justified in using deadly force only if he reasonably believes that that force is necessary to prevent serious bodily injury to himself or a third person or the commission of a forcible felony. No person in this state shall be placed in legal jeopardy of any kind whatsoever for protecting himself or his family by reasonable means necessary.

B. A person is justified in using reasonable force, including deadly force, against another person if he reasonably believes that the force is necessary to prevent or terminate the other person's unlawful entry of or attack on his dwelling or curtilage.

C. With respect to property other than a dwelling or curtilage, a person is justified in using reasonable force against another person if he reasonably believes that the force is necessary to immediately prevent or terminate the other person's trespass on or criminal interference with property lawfully in his possession, lawfully in possession of a member of his immediate family, or belonging to a person whose property he has the authority to protect. However, a person is not justified in using deadly force unless that force is justified under subsection (a) of this section.

D. Notwithstanding subsections (A.), (B.), and (C.) of this section, a person is not justified in using force if:

1. He is committing, or is escaping after the commission of a crime;

2. He provokes unlawful action by another person, with intent to cause bodily injury to the other person; or

3. He has entered into combat with another person or is the initial aggressor, unless he withdraws from the encounter and communicates to the other person his intent to do so and the other person nevertheless continues or threatens to continue unlawful action.

The law in your state may be quite different than the law stated above. That is why it is imperative that you research the law in your state. Many state statutes are now available on the Internet. A search there may provide you with the relevant statutes in your state. If not, most public libraries, college libraries, and certainly law school libraries near you will have your state's statutes. If you are unfamiliar with how to find the statutes, ask at the reference desk and they will point you in the right direction.

Now, with the caveat that the law may be different where you live, most self-defense statutes have a common principle; namely, that the force used be reasonable and necessary under the circumstances. If you are in a situation where the legal defense of self-defense is raised, the case is one where a jury or judge is going to consider whether the force you used was reasonable under the circumstances. In other words, was your response to an attack reasonable and necessary? Self-defense, in legal terms, is a legal defense raised either in a criminal prosecution or a civil damage case, which seeks to justify an act that would otherwise be a crime. For instance, if one person punches another person in the face, he may be guilty of assault and also responsible for certain civil damages. If, however, the punch was landed while trying to repel a violent physical attack, then the issue of self-defense will be raised, which may justify both the punch and the resulting injuries. The justification for punching back is to protect yourself (i.e., acting in self-defense).

"The justification for punching back is to protect yourself (i.e., acting in self-defense)."

As I have stated previously, the laws governing self-defense flow from and support the natural law, which gives every law-abiding person the unquestionable right to stay alive and to stay unharmed. One common misconception about self-defense is that when a person is violently attacked, he can only repel the attacker with force similar to what the attacker is using. For instance, many believe that if attacked with fists, a person must defend without the use of a weapon, or if attacked with a knife a person is limited to using similar types of weapons by law. As seen from the statute cited earlier, this notion is both wrong and dangerous.

The notion that we can only defend ourselves with "like-kind" force presupposes that the law places us on equal footing with our attacker. This is never true. You have the right to remain free from attack, and no one (assuming you are not provoking an attack) has a legal right to attack you. So, the rights of the attacker and the person being attacked are diametrically opposed. If you are acting without fault, in a place where you have the right to be, and have a good faith reason to believe that you are in real danger of death or great bodily harm, you have the right to use force to repel an attack. The attacker has no such rights. So, again, thoughts that we are under some duty to meet an attack with the same type of force that the attacker is bringing to us must be dismissed. Common sense dictates this as well.

For instance, imagine hypothetically that your mother is in her kitchen peeling potatoes when a 250-pound maniac kicks in the door and rushes her. Now, if she could only use the same amount of force in defending herself as the criminal clearly intends to use against her, she has little chance of surviving unharmed — which is always her right to do. She is surprised, probably outweighed, probably outmuscled. She is also the only person of the two who has an unequivocal right to be where she is and to be doing what she is doing. When her home is invaded and harm is imminent, there is no requirement that she play by the attacker's rules.

In self-defense cases, all the circumstances surrounding the attack, and the force used to stop the same, will be viewed to determine whether the use of force was proper and justified. The law generally allows a person to use that amount of force which she correctly or reasonably believes to be necessary for her protection. [See generally, Restatement (Second) of Torts section 70 1(1) (1965)]

In the hypothetical above, if the lady turns and uses her potato knife to put an end to the attack, and perhaps the attacker, who among us will say that she acted unreasonably? Probably no one.

Now that you have seen at least one state's law on self-defense and have an understanding of how the law justifies violence to counter violence, do this: Try to recall the last time you read in the paper or saw on the news a case wherein someone was claiming he acted in self-defense in doing whatever it was he did. What was your initial reaction to the story? No matter what your initial opinion, you no doubt felt more comfortable in stating that opinion once you learned more about what happened. That is, the more facts you knew, the more comfortable you were in believing the person was guilty or innocent of the crime charged. Right? The reason I want you to do this exercise of remembering what your gut feeling was when you heard the story is because whatever your initial reaction, what you were doing, without articulating it, was determining whether or not you believed the person acted reasonably under the circumstances.

Reasonableness, like someone's credibility, is either there or it isn't. In large part you were doing exactly what the law requires when viewing the subject of self-defense: Determining whether, under the circumstances, the use of force was reasonable.

In the United States there are at least three standards by which a person's use of force will be judged to determine whether it was reasonable. To discuss each of these three standards in depth, and how they differ from each other, would fill a book. I will touch on the standards by name though, if for no other reason than to alert you to the fact that different jurisdictions within the United States may judge your use of force differently.

The first standard is called the objective standard. In Langley v. State (1979, Alabama Appellate Court) 373 So 2d 1267, the court held that the conduct of the victim that would justify the exercise of the right of self-defense must be such as would manifest to the mind of a reasonable person a present intention to kill him or do him great bodily harm.

In essence, the objective standard asks: Would a reasonable person believe that the attacker in this particular case intended to kill her or do her great bodily harm? If the facts of the case lead to the conclusion that yes, a reasonable person would believe the attacker was going to kill or inflict great bodily harm, then the person who is claiming self-defense will be justified in doing what was done to repel the attack.

The second standard is called the subjective standard. Unlike the objective standard (which requires one to determine what some unidentified "reasonable person" would have believed), the subjective standard requires the jury to look directly into the mind of the person who is claiming to have acted in self-defense. In so doing, the jury attempts to determine the mindset of this individual at the time, and then the question becomes: Were the circumstances sufficient, in the mind of this person, to make her honestly and reasonably believe she had to use the force she used to protect herself from imminent harm? See the difference?

Objective — Would a reasonable and prudent person believe force was necessary to avoid serious injury or death?

Subjective – Did the person being attacked reasonably believe force was necessary to avoid serious injury or death?

Finally, the "discretion of the jury" standard. In a nutshell, this standard simply requires the jury to determine, from all the facts, whether or not the use of force was necessary to avoid serious bodily injury or death.

Although these standards differ somewhat, and in some places are used together to create a hybrid standard, the one constant throughout is that the action you take must be reasonable under the circumstances. To be characterized as self-defense the response must be in proportion to the danger. Broadly speaking, the person who uses force is not privileged to apply a particular force if he knows, or should know, that the harm can be prevented by applying a force less in kind and degree. This is in keeping with the general rule, as stated in the Restatement Second of Torts, cited here:

The actor is not privileged to use any means of self-defense which is intended or likely to cause a bodily harm... in excess of that which the actor correctly or reasonably believes to be necessary for his protection.

The author of this book confronts this point on a daily basis in his training of police departments across the country. In law enforcement terminology, the concept of reasonable force is referred to as the "force continuum." Simply put, in a street situation you can go from an arm- or wristlock (against the cantankerous town drunk) to... headbutts, knees and elbows in a life-or-death situation. Perhaps all the attacker needs to be dissuaded is the simple sight of someone up on his toes, moving, ready to fight. If so, great. The fight ended before it started. Perhaps, though, this attacker can only be dissuaded by pain. Whether this pain is inflicted through destructions of his punches and kicks, or through the message his groin sends his brain when it gets kicked is, in essence, his decision. Exactly what will he endure before he decides that you will not be prey? Perhaps the fight escalates to the use to weapons — a knife, broken bottle, stick, or whatever. If you have trained yourself to flow from range to range, empty hands to weapons, you will understand that you must do whatever is necessary to win against the attacker. If it means running from a knifefight, hey, you escaped and survived...which is the whole point here. If, on the other hand, it means drawing your knife and engaging the attacker, and "defanging the snake," great! A life-threatening situation was solved with a cut to the attacker's weapon hand. The weapon is gone, he decides to quit the fight, and you survived. Now leave!! Break contact and go report the incident to the police, giving them a description of the attacker and telling them he is very likely getting a cut on his hand stitched at the hospital.

"In the end, self-defense boils down to using common sense."

As I said at the beginning, the right of self-defense is very dynamic. Unlike many other things in the law, the right to self-defense is not limited by actualities, but by reasonableness of belief. Because of this, in rare instances we see cases where a person is justified by way of self-defense where he used such force as reasonably appeared necessary to repel the attack...even though, in retrospect, it was more force than was actually necessary.

In evaluating the person's conduct in such cases, all the facts and circumstances at the scene will be considered. The focus then will be on whether the circumstances which were known or should have been known to the person were such to create in him an honest and reasonable belief of being in danger of death or great bodily injury.

In cases where an attacker is seriously injured, and the defense of self-defense is raised, facts relevant to any jury consideration will include threats and/or overt acts of the attacker; the time and place of the occurrence; the fierceness or persistence of the assailant; whether the assailant actually had a weapon, or appeared to have a weapon; the age, sex, physical size and condition, as well as the strength of the assailant relative to the same information about the person who was defending against the attack. It is important to remember that, ultimately, if an attacker is seriously injured or killed and you are forced into court to explain your actions, the case will likely be decided by jurors who are ordinary folks, just like us. Because of this, they will naturally pay close attention to the facts surrounding the attack, and will always be more understanding of folks who repel an attacker in their home; while protecting loved ones; or going about their daily lawful activities. This is not to say that the defense of self-defense is unavailable to people who frequent known "tough bars or clubs" where fights break out on a regular basis. But remember, it is a natural question to ask why you were there, what you were doing, and whether or not you knew the reputation of the place and the people who gather there. This may not seem fair, but that is life. Ask yourself who you would initially feel more sympathy for: a mother who uses a knife to defend herself and her young child while walking in the park, or someone who does the same thing while drinking in a biker bar known for its knifefights? Both people may have been acting in self-defense, but one case has more difficulties than the other.

In the end, self-defense boils down to using common sense. If you go into a biker bar looking to test out your knifefighting skills, you are not likely to find sympathy or understanding from a jury in either a criminal or civil trial when you claim you were using the knife in self-defense. It is a much different case when a knife is used to prevent a would-be rapist from accomplishing his goals late at night in your home.

As we near the end of this chapter there is one other issue to address. I have heard, as I am sure you have heard, people say that, in effect, they would love to study martial arts but that if they did and got into a fight, they would be more liable than if they knew nothing. The response to this statement is twofold.

First, if you are attacked, the most important thing at that moment is knowing how to repel the attacker. Liability is not going to be on your mind at that point, nor should it be. Remember, the law gives you the right to stay alive and unharmed, using whatever means are reasonable to accomplish that goal. If you are attacked, the attacker is already a criminal...you are not. So, even if knowing how to win the battle for your life held the potential to make you liable to the attacker (and it doesn't), what is your option? Avoid potential liability by allowing the attacker to have his way with you, or with your family? Getting seriously injured or killed? Those are not sane options.

Secondly, knowledge legally gained does not magically transform you into some "liable" person. This subject always reminds me of a story told about a college professor who taught his doctoral class the "how-to's" of building and detonating a nuclear bomb. At the end of the lesson the professor turned to his students and said, "Now that you have the knowledge, what you do with that knowledge and how you use it will determine whether you are a scientist or a terrorist." So it is with the martial

> **"Remember, the law gives you the right to stay alive and unharmed, using whatever means are reasonable to accomplish that goal."**

arts. If you use your knowledge and skills to become a bully and a criminal, you will suffer the consequences of your actions. If, on the other hand, you use the knowledge that Paul Vunak has given thousands of law-abiding people to protect your life and the lives of your family members, the skills will be an irreplaceable asset.

Never allow anyone to dissuade you from learning to protect yourself. 911 is a great insurance to those covered by it, but what will you do in the three-to-15 minutes it may take for the police to respond? The cretins and perverts of society will not wait for the police to arrive, nor will they play by anyone's rules but their own. Do not be lured into a false sense of security that your alarm system, a barking dog, or 911 is going to save your life. These may help, but ultimately, your survival and well-being is in your own hands. Remember, you have the absolute right to stay alive and unharmed. Do what is necessary to keep that right.

Bruce Aukerman is an attorney in the state of Indiana.

CHAPTER 10

A Final Salute

It is said that a wise man learns from his mistakes. Well, a wiser man learns from someone else's. Contained within these pages (sometimes between the lines) are many of the mistakes I've made over the years.

I believe that intrinsic in the nature of a true teacher is the ability to step down off the "Grand Poobah" pedestal and communicate to others as a friend. I've learned that firsthand from Dan Inosanto over the past 24 years. And although the words in this book are mine, I will tell you now that the knowledge is Dan's.

Relaxing with Alfonso Tamez and Dan Inosanto.

Top row (left to right): Dell Pollard, Tim Tackett. In second row (from left): Paul Vunak, Chris Kent, Hal Falkner and Ted Lucay Lucay, In first row (from left): Dan Inosanto, Deby Frosto and Richard Bustillo.

Jerry Poteet, Paul and James Demile.

Author Paul Vunak (lower left) and his professional group of instructors and students who spent countless hours making sure the technique photographs were easy to understand and follow. Clockwise from left: Robert Kincaid, Eric Berger, James Wilks, Jeff Clancy, Steve Blatus, Erin Vunak, Tim Ballenger and Paul.

NOTES

NOTES

NOTES